Customising Your Electric Guitar.

Customising Your Electric Guitar.

by Adrian Legg.

&

Amsco Publications.
New York/London/Sydney/Cologne.

Cover design by Pearce Marchbank
Photography by George Taylor, Rembrandt Bros.
Properties by Ben Sutton

First published in Great Britain in 1981 by Kaye & Ward Ltd.
This edition published 1983 by Amsco Publications,
A Division of Music Sales Corporation, New York, NY.

International Standard Book Number: 0.8256.2262.X

Exclusive Distributor:
Music Sales Corporation
225 Park Avenue South, New York, NY 10003, USA

Contents

Acknowledgements

My thanks to Jim Wilmer and all at Rose Morris Ltd., who have remained patient and helpful in the face of my occasionally crackpot experiments, and their outraged neighbours.

My special thanks to Derek Baxter in particular, who stood on wobbly stools and generally got himself into some very uncomfortable looking positions to take the majority of the photographs for this project.

Thanks to electronics engineer, Colin Clark, who has frequently and patiently explained why things didn't / did / may or may not work.

Thanks to my wife, Di, who has put up with some astonishing nocturnal mumblings about switch location, and tolerated unusual smells emanating from the scullery workshop.

Thanks to Joanne and Joseph for not touching things, and leaving their father in peace at crucial moments.

My thanks also to the many people in the industry who have answered my questions and freely given good advice, among them Larry DiMarzio, Bill Kaman, Bill Davies and all the others at Ovation, Chas and Doug Chandler at Chandler Guitars, luthier David Bourne, luthier George Love, and Stephen Church at Stentor.

Adrian Legg

Foreword

The idea of this book is to pass on things I've found out or experimented with on a try it and see basis, partly in the search for a better sound for myself, and partly merely out of curiosity.

I came to it all originally simply as a musician with a particular musical bee in the bonnet, and think that money and effort spent on actually developing the machinery of your instrument is ultimately as valid a part of making music as money spent on lessons or books, and effort spent on practice. Having a good sound is inspiring and exciting, and having the technique to exploit or create it is essential. So customising is part of the old musical business of combining directly emotional ideas with the physical realities of an instrument. Whether you get a satisfying twang by sorting out your right or left hand technique or by rewiring your guitar, the satisfying twang is still the end goal.

It is perfectly possible to get sounds out of one guitar that are more usually associated with a completely different type, and still keep an option on the original. Switches and knobs are no substitute for good playing, and they cannot be used as crutches in the same way as effects pedals. Rather, the things they can be made to do can provide extra weapons for the armoury of a good player — some subtle, some dramatic.

Understanding and being able to alter your own guitar gives you, the player, the ability to decide how your music should sound and feel, and leaves you independent of the decisions of manufacturers. Manufacturers have to make many guitars the same, that's how they survive and how we get affordable guitars at all. Unfortunately, that process of mass production cannot take account of the musician who doesn't want to sound the same as everybody else. Hence the boom in custom parts.

Standard fitting replacement parts are available for most commonly used guitars, and most successful guitars have their design roots in one or other of two basic types, that is, Fender or Gibson, so standard screw-on or bolt-on bits like knobs or bridges don't require much explanation.

Brass parts may seem to be purely cosmetic at first sight, but my own experiments have convinced me that where they affect sound they affect it for the better. I have found that increasing mass at the bridge and fitting a brass nut has lifted performance, increasing sustain, and spreading it more evenly, and enhancing highs. So far nobody I know who has paid the price for the fairly expensive tremolo brass bridges has regretted it, though several have had to rethink their normal amp settings!

Apart from the bolt-on goodies, customising involves areas you can cope with with minimal experience and equipment, and areas that will require specialist skills. Where you differentiate between the two is a matter for your

One of my experimental brass plate 12 ounce bridges, which, in conjunction with strings run from the back of the guitar, lifted performance dramatically.

own confidence and competence. (See Notes for some of the tools.)

But you must be pretty good with your hands to be able to play the guitar at all, and I think that you'll find that there is quite a lot that you *can* do, so long as you can break with the good old British tradition of totally ignoring instructions until something has gone wrong.

Basic Set-Up

The neck should have a slight forward curve when under tension, called relief, and this can be measured using a straight edge (see Notes) and feeler gauges. It will show as a gap between the edge laid along the centre of the fingerboard and fifth to eighth fret tops of between five and fifteen thousandths of an inch, decreasing gradually on either side of the central maximum point. The maximum point may be higher up the frets on guitars with longer fingerboards. The theory and practical result is that this curve allows room for the vibration of the string, which forms a curve at the extreme points of its movement. If your neck were dead straight, you would not be able to get a reasonable action without bad rattles in lower positions, particularly from the bass strings. If you think about it, it follows that a harder player needs more relief than a light picker, and that there should also be slightly more relief on the bass side than on the treble. Where the latter actually occurs on mass production guitars, it is more likely to be by accident than design, and should occur naturally anyway by virtue of the slightly harder pull of the bass strings on the neck. If it is not apparent, don't worry too much as long as you have a good overall relief figure. The measurement must be taken with your strings tuned to normal playing pitch.

The necessary amount of relief is achieved by adjusting the truss rod. If the curve is too low, the truss rod nut must be unscrewed gently and the rod slackened. If you have too much of a curve, the rod

DiMarzio paduk / maple / mahogany body, ebony / maple neck. X2N pick-ups series / single / parallel and phase. Brass nut and bridge. Schaller machines. Finish is American, gloss styremica.

must be tightened. While your neck is actually quite strong, truss rod adjustment is a moderately delicate business, and should not be treated casually. Until you get a feel for and understand your particular neck, carry out any necessary adjustment a quarter of a turn or less at a time, with the correct truss rod key or wrench, and measure and observe carefully at each stage. Remember that the neck may take a while to respond to increased or decreased truss rod tension, so if you don't seem to be getting anywhere at first, stop adjusting and leave the guitar to settle for a while tuned to pitch. You can carry on playing it. Necks vary considerably in the way and speed with which they react, so take your time, and careful measurement and observation will keep you out of trouble.

A note of extreme caution must be added here. On a good quality electric with light gauge strings, it is possible to adjust the truss rod while the guitar is tuned to concert pitch, but still risky. This is not advisable on a heavy strung guitar or a bass, where the higher tension of the strings places a far greater strain on the truss rod, and consequently on the thread of the nut and the end of the rod. On a good quality guitar, the truss rod nut is usually made of brass, or a softer metal than the rod, so that if stripping should occur, it will happen to the nut rather than the rod. It is always safer to slacken the strings before making the adjustment, particularly on cheaper guitars, where one of the sacrifices involved in getting the price down may have been the quality of metal of the truss rod.

It is advisable to check that the truss rod nut and thread is not fouled with varnish. If it is, protruding thread should be cleaned out carefully with a fine point, and the area around the nut should be scraped clean. This is particularly so where the adjustment is by nut rather than hexagonal socket, as varnish blobs may prevent the socket of the adjusting tool from seating properly on the nut. I use dental tools (see Notes) for these and similiar scraping purposes, but a good quality scribe can be used, or an old small screwdriver with the blade tip bent to a curve and the sharp corners filed off.

It is of course, absolutely vital that you use the correct size wrench, as if you do foul up the flats and angles on nut or socket, there is virtually no room to get a locking gripper in at the headstock to remove the ruined nut. A very light touch of WD 40 or Castrol DWF on threads is always a good idea.

Truss rod replacement was always a perfectly feasible operation on traditionally built guitars where heat soluble glues were used. On modern solids, it is best always to behave as if spoiling the truss rod ruins the neck. A further point to watch for: if you lay the tuned guitar flat with the neck unsupported, the weight of the neck and headstock pulling back on the neck will decrease relief, and conversely, if you support it too high, the weight of the guitar pushing down will increase it. Be sure to allow for this when setting, and make your final measurements with the guitar in playing position. Relief can also vary slightly on lighter necks according to climatic conditions, and regular observation will teach you where to set to allow for this.

If the neck has too little relief, and is reluctant to come forward, leave the truss rod nut loose for up to a month, with maybe a blob of Blue Tac to stop it rattling when you play. If it still hasn't moved, consult a *reputable* repairman or the manufacturer, it may need a little heat treatment and clamping to remind it of what it's supposed to do. This obviously doesn't apply to guitars with push-pull truss rods, such as Shergolds, where simply undoing the truss rod nut forces the neck forward. Do bear in mind that many new guitars will have a very low relief figure at the start of their lives, and this will usually increase slowly as the neck settles in. On some, it is possible that a very slight backward lean will cure itself in the same way. This lean has usually come about as a result of the guitar being shipped or stored without any string tension. If it doesn't cure itself, again, consult the dealer or a repairman. Remember though, a badly bent back neck may well be incurable if it has been that way for a long while.

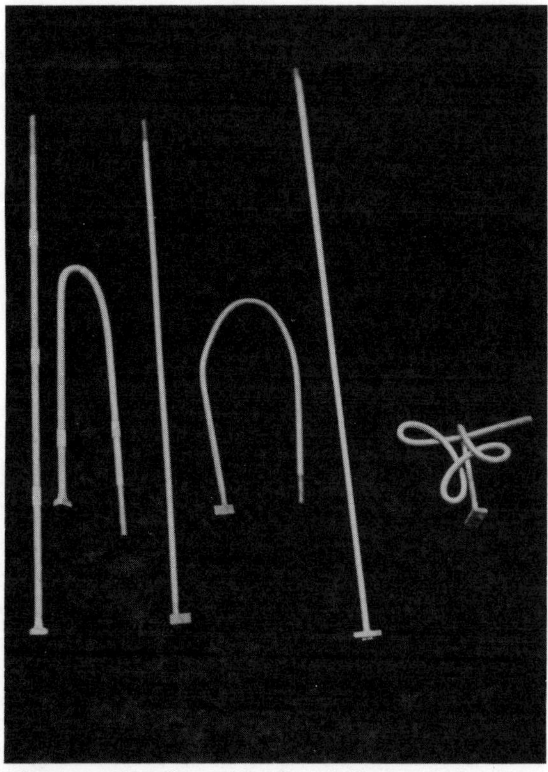

Three pairs of truss-rods, of obviously varying quality.

ACTION

Once you have your relief sorted out, you can set your action. Really, the practical absolute minimum you can go for on a low camber fingerboard, is about I.Imm treble 1.9mm bass. On a higher camber fingerboard, you won't be able to bend this without the string moving across the hump and cutting out. This height is measured where the string passes over fret twelve, between fret top and string bottom.

You will find that with Les Paul type bridges where the action is adjusted overall at either end of the bridge by either screw top poles or fingernuts under the bridge on threaded poles, you will need to slack the strings when adjusting the bridge height. On screw top poles, failing to do this may well cause you to damage the screw slots, as the metal is never particularly hard here. On finger-nut adjustment, you'll probably find that it is impossible to do it without slacking the strings, but even if you can, the bridge will move under tension on the threaded poles and may damage the thread. When fitting a replacement custom bridge unit, any filing or reaming of the holes that you may find necessary should be finished smooth with fine abrasive paper, and corners should be rounded off in order to protect the poles.

Where you intend to raise action at the bridge, remember that if the strings have been left at concert pitch, raising the bridge will increase string tension and pitch and could cause damage or breakage.

Individual saddles should also be adjusted with a slacker tuning again to protect the threads and worms, and should be adjusted so that they rest in a horizontal position. This is because on a close fitting unit, a tilt could disturb string spacing.

A light nick or groove can be made in the saddle to prevent sideways slipping where the angle of the strings over the saddle is not sufficient to prevent it. This should be deeper at the string ball end side of the saddle so that sideways restraint is done *behind* the point at which the string leaves the saddle and vibrates. This point must be cleanly finished, and there should be a positive, but not sharp, lateral bar to avoid buzzing. If you cut a deep V into the saddle, you will generate buzzing. Make sure that all the edges behind the saddle that the string will come into contact with are smooth, and that there are no angular points which could cause premature string breakage.

FRETS

You may not be able to achieve your lowest action without dressing your frets. First check to see that the frets are properly seated and not lifting out anywhere. If you suspect that they are loose, you should seek professional advice. If, however, the tops are uneven simply because of wear, or light buzzing is occurring at a few points when trying to set an action around the 1.1 to 1.3mm mark, then dressing may well be all that is needed.

The tops of the frets should be cut down *lightly* with a fine single cut ten to twelve inch flat file. A good quality file, undamaged, and checked for straightness, should be used, and the corners and handle tang should be ground off smooth to minimise possible damage from accidental bashes. Strokes should be even and light, and you will probably be able to feel the higher areas as the file drags more where it is cutting more. A few strokes should be enough to level out inconsistencies, and unless you are experienced, don't try to do much more than this.

When you have removed enough of the fret tops to solve the problem, the tops can be rounded off with a fret file. Various diameter concave cutting edges can be had now, and they do simplify things greatly. Again, light usage is the watchword, and once you've rounded off, the frets can be smoothed with 320, then 600 grit wet and dry, and polished up with either 0000 gauge steel wool or buffing soap and leather. The fingerboard and surrounding area is best taped throughout the operation. A quick solution to a single high fret is to use an Arkansas flat slip-stone, which will take the fret down very gradually and leave a relatively unscratched surface. This is only really a last minute pre-gig solution, and takes a bit of experience.

It also usually means, where the fret was sprung rather than unevenly worn, that that fret will eventually have to be replaced. Normal practice where a fret end is lifting out is to remove and reshape the fret. I use end cutters that have been ground flat, that is, the outside bevel cut down so the cutting edge will lie flush against the fingerboard.
These can be used, very carefully, to lift the fret out at the same time as pushing down against the fingerboard to help avoid tearing the wood. Once the fret is out, it can be tapped, with a chasing hammer or some other smooth faced hammer, back into a curve, and the tang, the bit that goes into the slot, can be nicked with the cutters to give a better grip on the slot sides. This operation may well be best left to the professional, as there can be many problems with frets and fingerboards that require experience. However, if the guitar is not particularly valuable, or the fingerboard is near the end of its life, this may present the opportunity for you to start acquiring some experience of your own. It is also possible, though bad practice, and really only for fingerboards that are badly worn, to tack a fret end down with a light dose of ethyl cyanoacrilate. See Glues.

Work on frets is very close to the area that requires professional experience, and if you wish to go further in this direction, this is where you should start thinking about picking yourself up a cheap or wrecked guitar to practise on. The abundance of Les Paul copies during the seventies, and the fact that Jap manufacturers have now gone more original, coupled with the recession, means that you should be able to get hold of something useful and capable of development very cheaply.

THE NUT

At the nut, I think it is fairly common for production guitars to have an action that is higher than necessary. Cutting the slots a little deeper to lower the strings is done with needle files. You will be able to see from the edges of the files available at

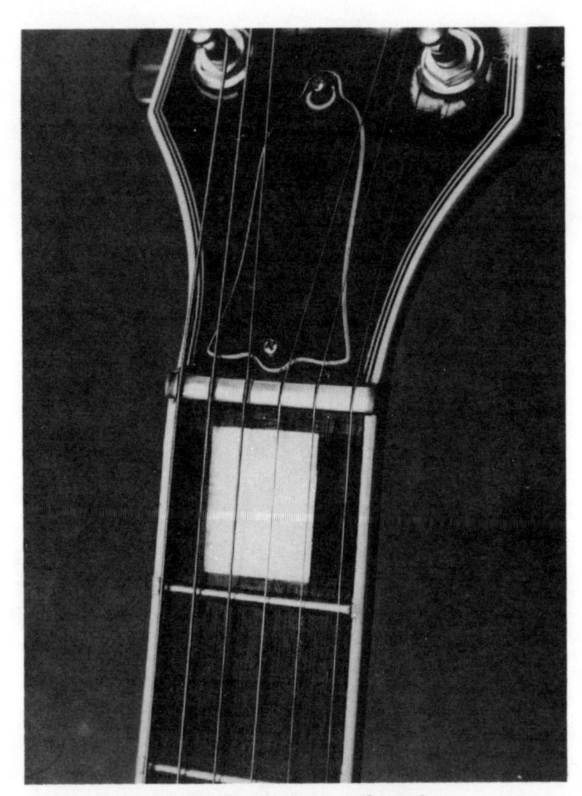

Brass nut, fitted, but not yet fluted.

your tool shop what sort of cut they will make, and a range of three or four small edge cutters will cover your basic needs. I have found it difficult to get fine enough knife files, and eventually only succeeded when I found a cabinet maker selling up some tools. You may have to use a very fine saw blade for the thinner trebles.

To set the lowest available action, hold the string down at the first fret, and look to see where the string measures up to from the top of the second fret, against a small rule. Your open string height over the first fret should be the same. Cut carefully, measuring frequently, until you reach this point. If however, you are going to play a lot of bottleneck, your action is probably best left a little high at the nut for the sake of the slide sound in lower positions. Once you've set the action to the height you need, take off all the excess over the strings, this makes for a cleaner looking job, and gets stuff out of the way of your left hand in low positions. I like to flute the nut, that is, to file down between the string slots with a half round needle file or a rat tail file. This is difficult to clean up on soft plastic nuts, but looks good on bone, and beautiful on brass.

Soft plastic nuts are best got rid of, they tend to cut response, and if you have a particularly lifeless first string and have yet to find a good reason why, a soft nut is probably to blame. I have used bone on electric, but prefer it for acoustic, and always go for brass on my own electrics. I have found that brass has lifted response and treble, and is generally more reliable. It is more practical in the sense that an accident that could crack or break a bone nut will merely dislodge

A fluted bone nut on an Adamas.

brass. Many manufacturers are now fitting brass nuts as standard, so it is not just my opinion that they are a better bet.

Fitting a replacement is easy enough. Try to remove your old nut whole, by tapping lightly on the end of a large screwdriver with the blade tip against the nut from fingerboard side, or at the end if it sits in a slot. . Usually, all that is holding it in is a small dab of glue, but it is worth inspecting the neck finish *first* to see if it laps over the ends of the nut. If it does, scrape if off gently with a small blade before you remove the old nut, and this will save tearing and cracking.

When you've got the old one out, put it on one side, and clean out the old glue from the slot. If you've lifted a binding end, glue it back down now, and wait for it to set before you go on any further. Try the new blank for size, and where necessary, file the extra width off before fitting. You should also fine finish the ends before fitting, using, for brass, 600 grit wet and dry, then burnishing paste, or buffing soap and leather.

Use a very small dab of epoxy to cement the new nut blank into the slot, and wait for it to harden fully. When it is cured, tape up either side of the nut, and file it down roughly to shape. Take your old nut, and holding it against the new one, mark out the slots and cut them carefully. Setting it up fine is as before, and finish with 600 wet and dry and paste or soap as before. It obviously makes sense to cut as little of the slot as possible until you've got your strings on for checking action height, and you'll probably find you need to remove the tape over the fingerboard to measure accurately. I find it is a good idea to tape up the headstock thoroughly, and to grind off the points of the needle files, as it is easy to slip when cutting, and dig the point into the headstock finish and timber, particularly where the headstock does not lean back.

If you use tremolo, detune frequently, or use pre-set banjo pegs (see section on Keith pegs) you will find that lubricating the nut slots will allow a smoother drop and/or return of pitch. I've had consistently good results using Moly GN, which is a molybdenum disulphide paste marketed by Abbey Supply Co., 6 Mill Lane, Wallingford, Oxon., and sold in gunsmiths in 25 gram tubs for permanent dry lubrication of trigger mechanisms etc., This size will cost around a couple of pounds, and will last a good while as you only need to use minute quantities.

SETTING INTONATION

This requires a good ear and peace and quiet, or a guitar tuner with an indicating meter.

The guitar, being a fretted instrument, is out of tune with itself anyway. Laying out the frets to suit all keys is a mathematically equal process which gives perfect pitch to no one key, but a roughly equal degree of out-of-tuneness to all. On a valve amp, it is unlikely that you will notice this much, but it can be a pain on transistor amps. There is nothing much you can do about it, and you'll probably find that you unconsciously bend to compensate quite naturally.

Having got that out of the way, you can set your octaves spot on, as the twelfth fret bisects the scale length, and the halfway harmonic bisects the string length.

Play the harmonic at the twelfth fret, and then the note fretted at the twelfth fret. If the fretted note is flat relative to the harmonic, it means that the length from the twelfth to the bridge is longer than it should be. It must be shortened by moving the saddle forward until the pitch of the fretted note comes up to the pitch of the harmonic.

If, on the other hand, the fretted note is sharp relative to the harmonic, it means that the distance from the fret to the saddle is shorter than it should be. In which case the saddle must be moved back away from the frets until the pitch of the fretted note drops to equal that of the harmonic.

Scale lengths for each string vary according to thickness. The thicker a string is, the more it has a tendency to vibrate at a point slightly forward of the saddle, as it is restrained by its own thickness. Scale length adjustment also compensates for the fact that as you push a string down to the fret, you bend it out of true, and different strings on the guitar bend pitch at a different rate.

Care must be taken setting the intonation on the lower strings of a guitar which has pick-ups with magnetic polepieces, as the proximity of the magnetic field to the string can interfere

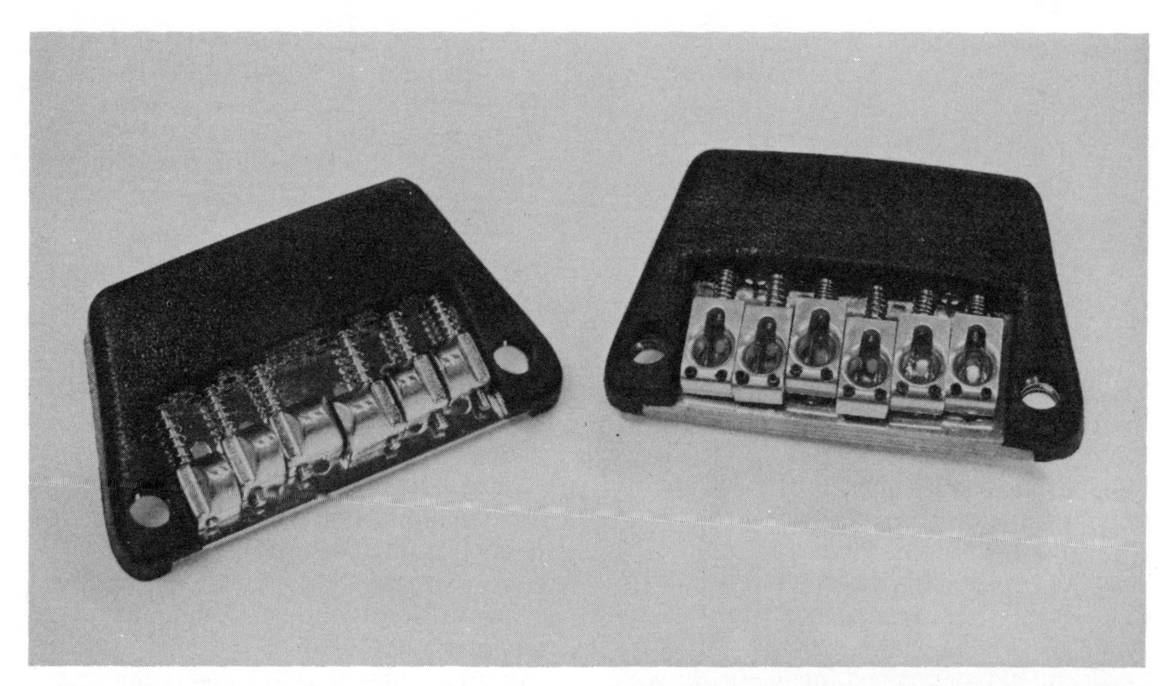

with its free vibration, and give a double note. If you set to allow for the double note, you may well find that lower positions on that string are out, as they are less affected by the magnetic pull.

Where the strings run over the saddle at an acute angle, moving the saddle back can increase string tension quite suddenly. On any bridge, it is worthwhile slacking the strings during adjustment to minimise pressure on, and consequently damage to, the adjusting screws.

In the picture here, the original Ovation bridge on the left has the strings run from the end over solid brass block saddles. The experimental bridge on the right has been drilled to bring the strings through from the back of the guitar over Tele type saddles, consequently the string angle over the saddles is much more acute. Intonation adjustment on both is effected from the rear of the unit by means of six sprung screws.

This shows the intonation screws at the back of the experimental bridge and the extra plates which helped lift top and alter sustain characterisitcs.

Glues

Traditionally, bone glue is associated with instrument making, and vile smelling stuff it can be too. A boil-up can be a nauseating experience, and should not be done in a home. The advantage of the stuff is primarily that a hardened joint is simple to open using a hot putty or palette knife and / or controlled amounts of hot water or steam. A tube from the end of a kettle spout can be used for the latter very easily. Heating this glue is done professionally with an electric glue pot, I was lucky and got an old one from a closing down factory, but an old saucepan and a spirit stove will do, unless you have an old electric ring that can be run in an outhouse or a sheltered part of the garden. Seriously, the smell can be a huge problem. You will encounter bone glue on traditionally built acoustic guitars more than anything else, where the need to repitch the neck as the guitar ages or the need to replace worn bridges make it ideal. You are very unlikely to find it on a production solid, but you may find it very useful for your own alterations / additions. A job will usually set hard within twenty-fours hours, and the glue is best bought in pearl form, powders have been known to be unreliable. It mixes one-two with water, and water can be added to an old batch to freshen it up. Spills and excess are easy to clean up with warm water. If you do use it, remember that a very warm temperature and high humidity will weaken it — a guitar I knew that went to South America whole came back in several pieces.

Epoxy compounds are now a part of everyday life, and on a modern solid, and indeed, many modern acoustics, you are more likely to come into contact with them, or, increasingly, a cyanoacrilate, or a white wood glue. Many white glues that are commonly available can creep, I rarely use them on anything except a wobbly kitchen chair. Epoxy compounds can be difficult to break open, and rough handling opening an epoxy joint can lead to damage. I have used some of the compounds available through industrial sources, and many are quite sophisticated, offering a range of viscosities and cure times that will suit varied applications, but I have found that a simple one to one fast cure epoxy copes with most problems in customising work. Epoxy will glue wood very satisfactorily and has good filling properties. Excess should be left to cure partially to a rubbery state, it can then be trimmed with a sharp knife.

If you try to clean it up too soon, it will smear. I have successfully cleaned soft smears off finishes with meths, followed by a good rub with a wax based polish. You don't need large quantities for jobs, but where you suspect you may get an ooze, mask off adjacent finished areas thoroughly first. If you try to clean up an ooze too late you may find that it has cured hard. Careful chipping may remove bigger lumps, but if it's only a small amount, it's probably best left alone.

The most fascinating glues around nowadays are the cyanoacrilates. I use two basic types, ethyl cyanoacrilate, which is mainly suitable for rubbers and plastics, and methyl cyanoacrilate, which is more suitable for metals and glass. I use a medium viscosity ethyl, a low viscosity methyl which is superb for close fitting metalwork and has a very high shear strength, and a high viscosity methyl which will fill gaps up to a ten thousandth of an inch according to manufacturers claims, but which I have found to fill bigger gaps where a high shear strength isn't essential. The high viscosity stuff will work very well on wood in conjunction with an activator spray, and I have found the eythl useful, among other things, for tacking down an occasional sprung fret end. The fact that it is not the most suitable for a metal to wood join means that getting the old frets out for a refret is not a severe problem provided that very small quantities are used. Generally speaking, I've found that it has only been necessary to use it on a fingerboard that is already pretty well shot up. Incidentally, it's worth mentioning at this point that a loose or poorly seated fret will kill off sustain, and a duff note in this respect gives a good clue as to what is wrong.

In general, it is best to assume that a suitable cyanoacrilate on well mating surfaces will be permanent. You will not be able to break it without causing damage elsewhere. As partial cure can take place in a few seconds, you will not have time to manoeuvre a piece once it has been applied, positioning must be precise and fast.

When used with an activator spray, full cure times are reduced considerably, and this can make these glues dangerous. At the moment of cure, they give off heat, and a blob on a fingernail suddenly curing can give you a nasty little surprise. Conversely, a small blob applied to a broken nail (without activator) can get you through a gig, but don't scratch for ten minutes immediately after application.

Cyanoacrilates are generally available now under a few trade names, and a chat with a good toolshop or hardware salesman should sort out what will suit your purpose best.

These glues cure by absorbing atmospheric moisture, so if you have a spill, flood it and clean up the cure after, don't try to wipe it up, you'll just stick the cloth to it. It is said on virtually all the tubes and packets, but it's worth saying again — skin to skin contacts with cyanoacrilate bond virtually *immediately*. If you can't get a skin bond into warm soapy water right away to ease it gently apart, you will need medical help. There is a fairly healthy store of legend building up about people turning up at medical centres with various things stuck to them at various points, but it's not actually very funny when it happens to you. If you suspect that a job could be tricky or messy, get the warm soapy water handy before you start, and condition yourself not to scratch or touch your face while you're doing it.

Remember, whenever you're gluing, try all the bits and the cramps together first dry — you don't want to discover that it won't work when you've got curing glue all over the place.

If your experience with any glue is limited or non-existent, then you really must try the glue out on scrap material with similar surface characteristics to the eventual job first. You may well find it safer, for example, to go for a slow cure glue than a fast cure. The advantages are that you will have more time to adjust things and clean up. The disadvantages of a slow cure glue are the possible difficulties of adequate cramping. You can't really sit there and hold the job together for several hours while it glues, so if in doubt, you should try out all the cramping arrangements before you even choose the glue. Remember, wedges, weights, strong elastic bands and bulldog clips can all be pressed into service in this cause, and if you are doing a long cure glue job in a family home, let everyone else know what is going on so that the job isn't moved or dusted in your absence. If you have children about the place, then obviously you must take extreme precautions to see that they don't get their hands on some of these materials.

Finishes

Where the fingerboard is not lacquered, rubbing refined linseed oil into the wood will help save it from drying out and splitting, and regular use, say about every two months, will keep it healthy enough to save undue tearing when the worn frets eventually have to come out. Refined linseed oil is available from fine art supply shops.

Teak oil is a possible finish, and while it can leave a neck feeling pleasantly woody, lighter woods can look a bit grubby after a while. Initially, the wood should be sanded down, and the oil brushed on liberally. After fifteen minutes, wipe off the excess, and sand down lightly with flour grade glasspaper. A second coat should then be applied sparingly with a cloth, and the surplus wiped off after five minutes with a clean cloth. This will give a matt finish, and maintenance is simply a matter of periodic re-oiling.

Linseed oil is another possibility. Raw oil should be spread over the bare wood, and left to soak for a few hours. The surplus should then be cleaned off, and the wood left to dry. If the surplus is not wiped off, it will form a rubbery gloss that will have to be scraped off. Drying will take several days, and the process must be repeated four or five times. After a few weeks at it, when the wood is finally dry from the last coat, it can be rubbed up to a dull gloss with a coarse rag. Linseed oil can be diluted three-one with pure turps, and this will speed up drying somewhat.

Waxing can be done, either on its own, or following linseed oil. A simple polish can be made up using shredded beeswax (I use a cheesegrater) dissolved in pure turps with a little boiled linseed added. If used, this must be rubbed in thoroughly, or it will feel tacky or greasy.

Bear in mind that using an oil finish can make lacquering very difficult later on. Although it is accepted practice to use linseed oil lightly under a lacquer finish to bring out grain, it must be rubbed down very hard and thoroughly before lacquer will stick. It could well be impossible to get lacquer to stick on a wood that has been well waxed — removing traces of the wax could involve quite substantial sanding down.

With lacquers, basically nothing will come out as well as a professionally done spray finish. Spraying takes skill and experience, can be very messy, and can seriously damage your lungs if you fail to take adequate precautions. If you intend to experiment, make sure you wear a face mask and have adequate ventilation. Don't go near the job you want to do well until you've spent at least a month pottering about spraying odds and ends to get the feel of the tool. Airless guns can be used to get reasonable results with experience, but viscosity will be crucial if you are to avoid spotting. Airless guns can also be phenomenally noisy, and enraged neighbours aren't going to help much. If you are intending to do a lot of spraying, then you are probably already investigating the cost of compressors, airlines and guns. Generally speaking, you will be very lucky to get a decent instrument quality finish with aerosol lacquers. The problem with these on small jobs particularly is that cleaning the nozzle after spraying requires you to discharge propellant gas. If you are doing lots of small sprays, you will end up with insufficient pressure and spotting will occur. A few years ago, I got quite reasonable colour results using car touch up spray cans, but I wouldn't really recommend it.

Polyurethane, suitably thinned, can be applied by brush, and here again I've had reasonable results doing thin and many coats, sanding between each one. It is probably most suitable as a light sealer.

I have had excellent results with brushes using melamine (see Notes), a two part type finish consisting of an ethanol mixture with acid catalyst which sets very hard and fast. It will go on over the top of polyurethane quite happily, and stick. It can be sprayed, and very well indeed if the viscosity is lowered with thinners. Cellulose thinners can be used for cleaning up tools but not for thinning,for this you must buy the special thinners.

When applying by brush, the bulk of the work is in the cutting back and buffing. I cut back with 320 grit wet and dry, then 600. If you have a drill and a bench mounting, you can buy a cloth edge buffing wheel and a pigtail to fit it quite cheaply. The pigtail is a threaded device with a very fast taper which will push into the cloth centre hole and grip it. You must buy so that the direction of rotation screws into the cloth. Using plenty of buffing soap on the edge, the buffer will take the chore out of it all, but must be used gently — too long and hard on one area will cause heating and blistering. Combine this with handrubbing with burnishing paste, then acrylic polish or metal polish, and finish off on a normal rotary polishing bonnet.

Make sure that the top of the buffing wheel rotates towards you, so that if the work is pulled, it is pulled down. Wear goggles or safety glasses, bits of buffing soap will fly off, and your eyes will be directly in the line of fire if you're watching what you're doing properly. The finish itself dries very quickly, and in a warm dry atmosphere, you can usually get a next coat on in two hours. If you're going to build up a few thick coats to get the bulk, leave it a little longer. Topping off with thinner coats will take some of the weight out of the sanding and buffing.

On many of the good quality replacement necks and bodies around now, there is already a good primary coat, and very often the guitar can look pretty good with no further finish. I have two particular bodies both the same, made of a blend of nicely coloured timbers, one has been sprayed a deep gloss, the other left with just a light primary coat or two, frankly the latter is the better looker as it looks more natural. So a heap of gloss isn't always the best idea, wood shouldn't look like plastic.

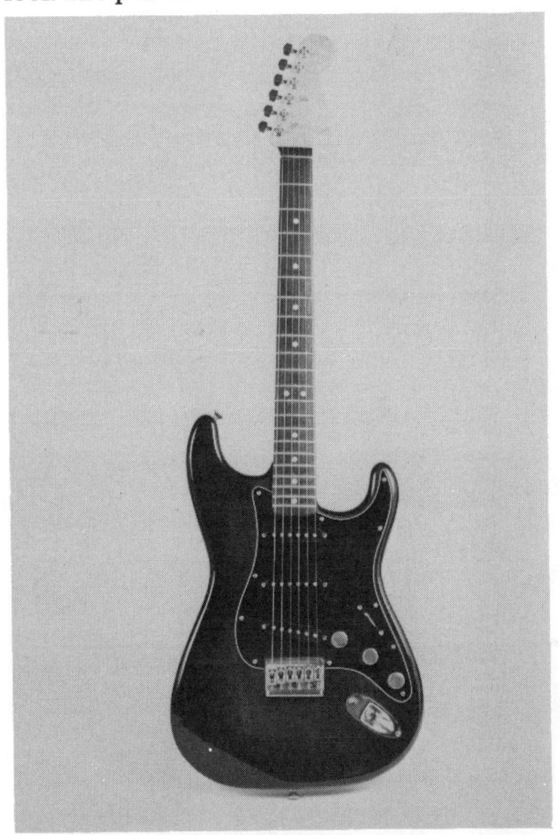

This guitar belongs to DiMarzio. It has 3 FSI's, five-way switch, brass fittings and DiMarzio neck and body.

Wiring

All you need is a soldering iron, a bit of commonsense, and a few simple tools.

The iron. Fifteen watts will be ideal — not too hot — for most fine wiring, but you may well find that it isn't hot enough to do the backs of pots. Twenty-five watts and upwards, and you will be able to cope with soldering on larger areas of metal, but you'll have to be very deft, and careful with heatsinks, on wire, and components like capacitors.

Heatsinks. I've used crocodile clips and they've worked. I also use small surgical forceps (see Notes) which clamp together. I put the end of the wire into the jaws, close them, apply solder to the end, and then use the forceps to put the wire against, or through the hole on the bits I want to attach it to, and then apply a little more heat from the iron. The forceps, as well as acting as a very good heatsink, keep my fingers well clear of the hot iron tip.

If you are going to put extra switches in, most of the suitable DPDT (Double Pole Double Throw) and SPDT (see Notes, Single Pole Double Throw) switches that you will want to use have quarter inch shafts, So you'll need a small hand-drill and a quarter inch bit. Switches can be had either from your dealer or your local electrical parts stockist.

If you are going to put switches into a control compartment which has access from the rear of the guitar rather than onto a scratchplate, you may well need a small carving gouge to take out a little wood around the inside end of the hole so that the switch will seat properly and the shaft project enough to get the nut and washer on. Mark out the area you're going to cut.

Drilling. I drill a small ($\frac{1}{32}$or $\frac{1}{16}$inch) pilot hole through from the inside first, which helps with internal location, checking for space etc., and then drill the quarter inch hole from the outside using the pilot hole as a centre. Done carefully, this doesn't harm the guitar's finish.

Allow yourself plenty of time to do a job, and just go over in your mind what you're going to do before you start. Don't be nervous of it, just careful, it's not open heart surgery and your guitar won't die in agony if you make a mistake. Don't rush, use your head, and you'll have no problems you can't solve.

PICK-UP BASICS

A single coil pick-up consists of a coil wound around a bobbin, and in the centre of the bobbin are either six magnets, one bar magnet, or six poles that conduct the magnetic field from a magnet underneath the unit. The wires at each end of the coil are connected to either two separate stronger wires, or to a single conductor and shield — a piece of co-ax.

The vibration of the strings over the pick-up excites the magnetic field and generates a minute *alternating* electric current, the frequency of alternation of which is exactly related to the frequency of vibration, or pitch, of the note being played on the strings. This current is your signal, and needs a normal complete electrical circuit to operate.

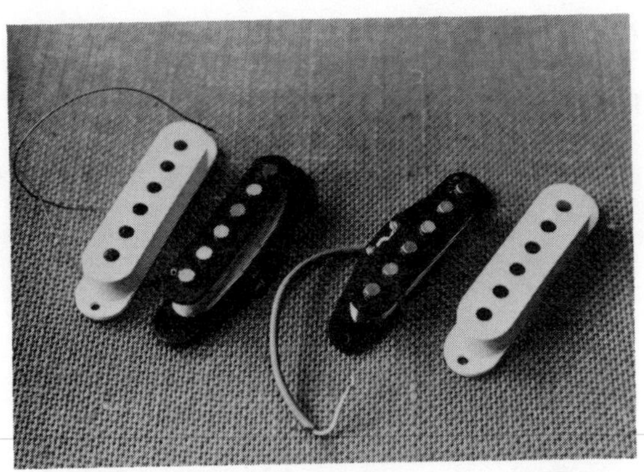

A couple of Jap single coil pick-ups — different makes, but both surprisingly good quality.

The variation in the number of wirings, type of magnet and so on, give the pick-up its tonal character. Pick-ups are also available that allow you to switch on or off part of the coil and vary the power and tone accordingly.

I'm not going to advise on the choice of type or make, that is entirely up to you, except to mention that pick-ups with the magnets set into the bobbin, while they may be tonally desirable, can cause problems by exerting a magnetic pull on the strings, and giving a 'double-note' sound on higher positions, particularly on the sixth and higher on the fifth. The only cure for this short of changing the pick-up is to sacrifice some power and lower it.

Some makers have used magnetic pole-pieces in humbuckers, notably Ovation, who claim a considerable extra noise reduction for their pick-ups, and the 'double-note' occurs on these guitars to greater or lesser extent. Basically, the stronger the magnetic field, or the closer it is to the string, the more likelihood there is of getting the double-note. Many players are quite happy to live with it for the sake of the tonal qualities, for others it is an irritant.

Fitting a phase switch on a single coil pick-up requires a simple two conductor lead, and not single and shield, which must be unsoldered and replaced. Shielding should be on the guitar itself, and all internal cavities should be lined with either a tough foil, or a commercially available copper shielding tape. All joins should be soldered together, and the whole should be connected to the earth at the jack socket, either directly or via the rest of the guitar earth. This shielding is especially important if you are going to play anywhere over low volume — an unshielded guitar will be very noisy and subject to the nastier bits of feedback once it is hooked up to a stack.

For the sake of simplicity, coils throughout the book will be drawn like this:

figure 1

represents coil ›

conductors

If you intend fitting new conductors to a pick-up, you'll find that by looking closely at the coils and connections of the old conductors that it is quite easy to see and differentiate between the opposite ends, and to match them on the two coils of a humbucker.

A humbucker consists of two coils wired in series and *out of phase*, over a magnetic field that varies from maker to maker. Here, I'm not concerned with the magnetic field, but with the alteration of the wiring to get different sounds, and so it's worth going over it to try and get a clearer picture of what it all means, particularly the out of phase bit.

As experienced players, we tend to associate 'out of phase' with the honky sort of sound given by two pick-ups operating together in a mix, but with the output of one coming from the opposite end of the coil/s to the other. That is, the phase of one is completely (electrically) reversed in relation to the other.

An apparently similar quality of tone can be obtained from a single humbucker (with a corresponding drop in volume) by running the coils together in series and *in* phase. This is the sound that most of us would call 'out of phase', and the sound of a normally wired (out) humbucker, because of its tonal quality, we tend to think of as sounding 'in phase'.

For the purpose of the wiring diagrams in this book, which after all, are to help to get different sounds, not teach you electrical theory, I'll refer to the usual humbucker wiring as normal coil phase, and the actually in, but sounding out, as reverse coil phase. If you do find that you have a coil phase problem after doing a bit of switch wiring, all you need to do is swap round the two wires from one of the coils anyway.

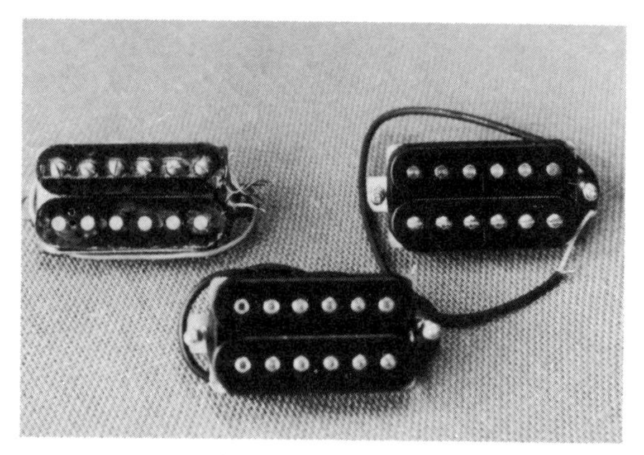

Three different Jap humbuckers — cheap and ideal for early wiring experiments.

If you are going to rewire an existing humbucker from single and shield to three of four conductor, the phase of the coils will need careful study. In some humbuckers, the out of phase wiring is achieved by winding the coils in opposite directions, in others, simply by running the output from one into the equivalent wire end on the other. The diagrams in this book assume the latter, but if your pick-up has opposite wound coils, then simply turn the bottom half of the diagram upside down and re-colour code accordingly.

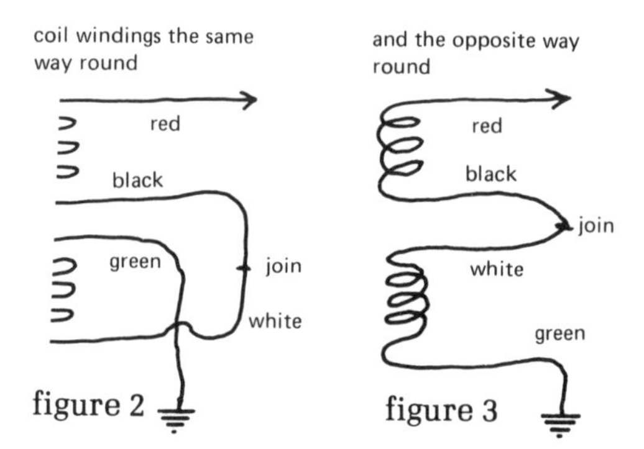

figure 2

figure 3

HOW PICK-UPS AND POTS WORK

As the volume is turned down from ten, output is weakened as current from the pick-up is taken from further and further round along the resistance, until at zero, the wiper (see Notes) is right by the earthed leg of the pot. Then the whole of the resistance is between the pick-up input and the wiper, and there is no resistance between the wiper and earth, so the output wire is earthed.

The tone control's job is to allow a varying amount of current through the capacitor, which will allow high frequencies through to earth. When the tone control is at ten, because the input is wired to the opposite leg than it is on the volume pot, the whole of the resistance is between the input and the wiper, so no current can pass. As it moves round towards the input when the control is

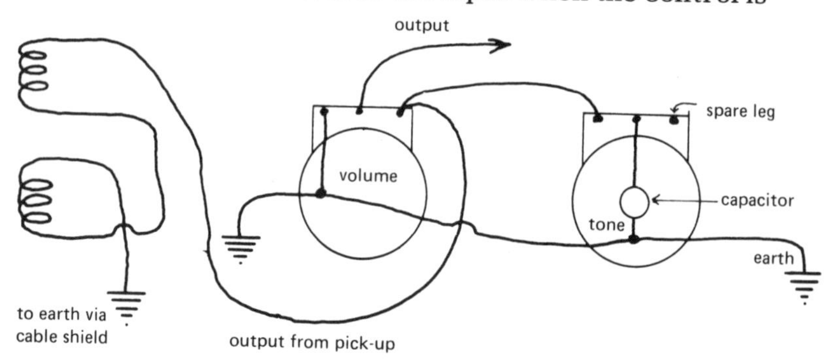

figure 4

turned down from ten, gradually less resistance is between the current and the earth, so an increasing amount of high frequency current (treble) will filter off to earth through the capacitor. Normal capacitor values on a guitar are either .05 microfarads or .022. The higher the figure, the further down the frequency range the tone control will cut.

These controls can be wired in different ways. For instance, the capacitor may be between the volume pot and the tone pot instead of the wire, and the centre leg of the tone pot will then be connected to earth. Or the capacitor could be connected to the top left leg of the tone pot and earth, and the wire from the pick-up would go to the tone pot centre leg.

On many two pick-up guitars that have separate volume and tone for each pick-up, when both pick-ups are selected, turning one volume right off will turn the other pick-up off as well. More often than not, this is an advantage to a player who wants to be able to shut the guitar off altogether now and then, and it provides a quick way of doing it.

However, if your guitar does this and you don't want it to, it can be rewired very simply.

Here, the output of each volume pot comes from the wiper, leg 2, which rotates over the resistance inside the pot. When the volume is turned right down, the wiper is right at the end of leg 3's side of the resistance. Leg 3 is earthed, so the output wire, and anything connected to it, like the other pick-up via the selector switch, will be earthed too.

If you swap the pick-up wire and capacitor on each channel from leg 1 to leg 2, and the output wire from leg 2 to leg 1, when the volume of one pick-up is turned right down, the pick-up itself will be earthed, and the whole of the resistance will be between the leg 3 earth and the output wire, so the other pick-up will not be affected.

figure 5

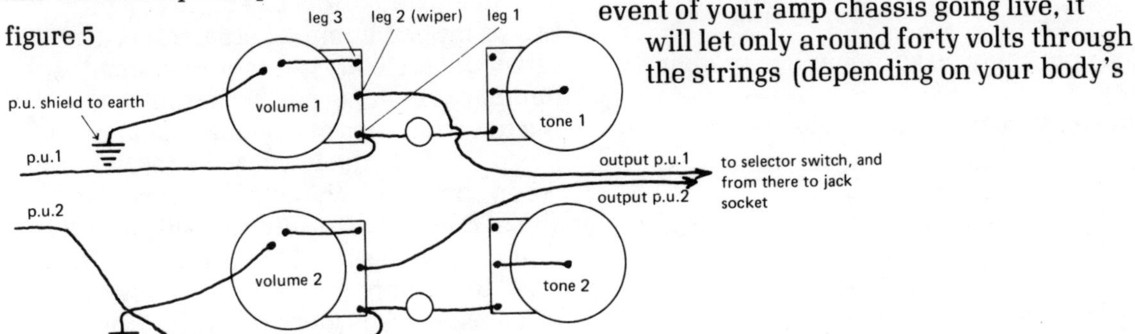

A Simple Safety Feature

On any good quality guitar, you will find a wire running from the bridge to the earth side of the guitar's wiring. This is the string earth, and is essential for cutting down serious hum and extraneous noise, and you can add this item to replace it altogether.

Wire together in parallel, a 220k ohm resistor (coloured bands red, red and yellow, and silver or gold which denote tolerance — gold is a closer tolerance and more expensive) and a .001 capacitor with a minimum voltage rating of 500 volts. Twist the wires together and then solder, like this:

figure 6

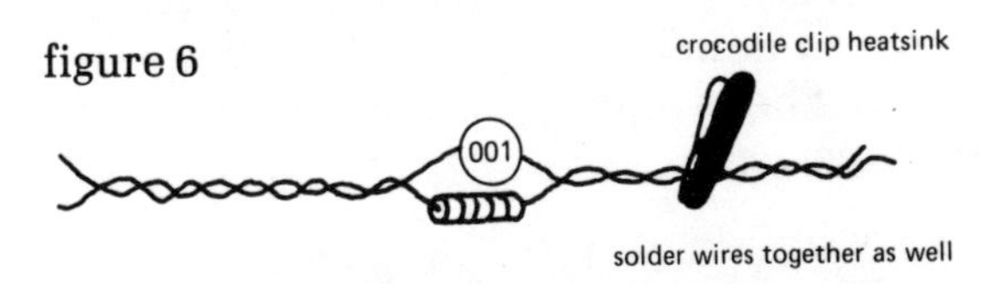

This unit should then be wired *inside the guitar* in between the bridge or tailpiece and the earth side of the circuit *replacing the string earth wire.* In the event of your amp chassis going live, it will let only around forty volts through the strings (depending on your body's conductivity), enough to give you a warning tingle without hurting you. It will allow enough leakage through for the string earth to operate normally. Obviously it will not stop things like your jack socket plate and switches going live, but you should have enough warning to be able to switch off at the mains before any harm is done.

Really, this should be regarded as an extra where safety is concerned, and where you are using powerful gear with a big mains consumption, you should use a mains trip system that will cut the current fast when a potentially dangerous fault occurs.

Cutting Treble Loss from Volume Pot

Many guitars lose their treble edge as the volume is turned down, and the .001 capacitor has a role to play in combating this. If it is connected between the in and out legs of the volume pot, it will allow high treble frequencies to bypass the pot altogether. The tone control will still cut them as normal. It can unbalance the sound a little sometimes. I have never found this a problem, a friend has, but I think you'll find it a cheap enough one to try out. I have found it very useful with coil taps.

figure 7

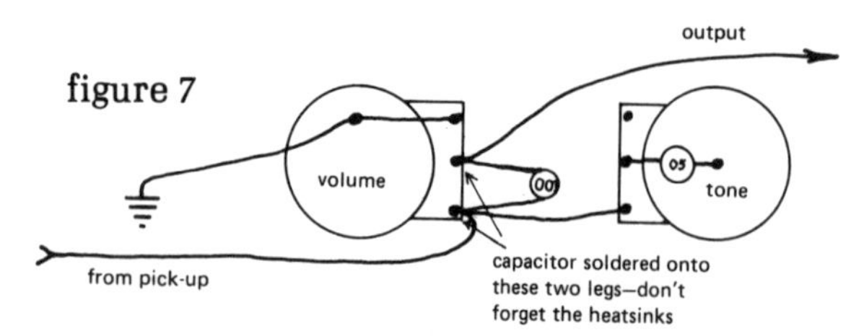

Your pots may be wired up the another way,
but the principle is the same.

figure 8

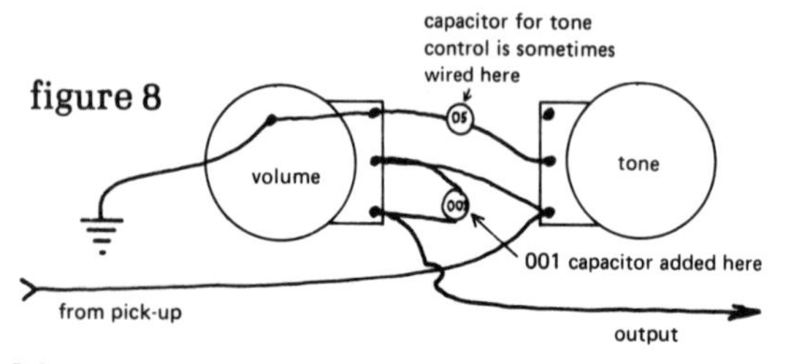

Switchable .001

If you've tried the .001 capacitor, and find it a help for some things and a hindrance for others, the answer is to make it switchable, using a Single Pole Double Throw mini-toggle switch. Incidentally, if you have a treble boost on your amp., and it seems to be less effective at higher volumes, this is probably how it works.

figure 9

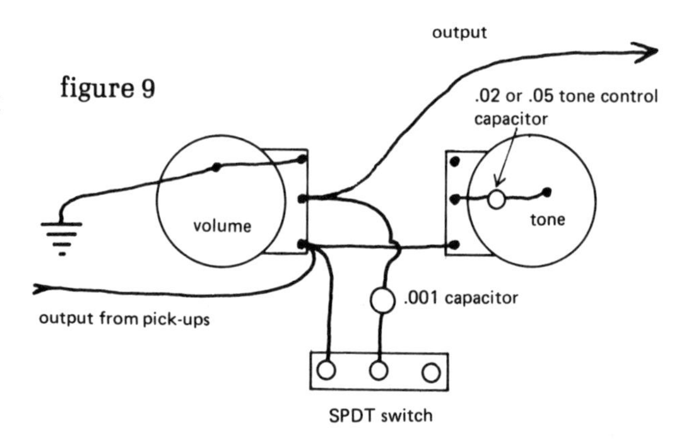

Generally speaking, I've found that noticeable treble loss occurs more with log. or audio pots, and happens quite positively around nine. It is less noticeable with linear pots, as the resistance change is smoother, but, in my opinion, linear pots can be less effective than audio for normal guitar use, and I have found a pair of linear volume pots virtually useless immediately in front of a pre-amp in the guitar. The effect of a .001 can be much more sudden on cheaper pots, but generally on a reasonable quality audio pot, will give a noticeable sharpening up effect on single coil pick-ups or tapped humbuckers at nine. The effect of treble lift is less pronounced with humbuckers in normal series output, and the tonal balance stays more constant down towards the lower volumes, where it can sharpen right up just before the signal cuts out altogether. A side effect is that normal passive tone controls will seem to be more effective, as at lower volumes, there is more treble left for them to cut.

BIASED MIX

This circuit takes advantage of treble loss to give a mix, at lower volumes, that is biased in favour of the bridge pick-up by virtue of the fact that the treble frequencies from that pick-up dominate. The .001 capacitor on the bridge pick-up circuit operates normally, allowing treble to bypass the pot. On the fingerboard pick-up however, it only comes into operation when the pick-up is selected solo. Consequently, when both pick-ups are selected and volume is reduced, the fingerboard pick-up will suffer treble loss, and the bridge pick-up will have enhanced highs. If you remember some of the older *"Fender" *"Telecaster" guitars, the fingerboard pick-up gave a muffled sound, which, mixed with the very trebly bridge pick-up, gave a sound which had weight and body, a strong back pick-up top end, but none of the sweet straight pick-up mix top end. Personally, I loved that sound, and this circuit can help take you some way towards it. It forms a part of the circuit I designed for the Vox Custom 25 guitar, where it has proved very effective. The effect is more dramatic on some cheaper tandem audio pots, where the normal treble loss occurs very suddenly at nine. Back pick-up positioning will generally decide exactly what tone you are going to get. I have found that using an .02 tap on the rear coil with the foremost coil 55mm from the first saddle centre, and using a straight muffled humbucker in the front, the tone has very similar Dobro like qualities to a *"Fender" *"Stratocaster" guitar 'out of phase' mix. This wiring is much more effective than simply using a tone control to cut highs on one pick-up, as the tone control will tend to cut highs from the whole mix.

COIL TAP

The neatest way of dropping out one of two coils in a humbucker to get a coil tap sound is simply to earth the link between the two. This means that both ends of one coil will be earthed, and that the remaining coil, the one nearest the hot wire, will have an earth. Switching the earth tap in and out can be done in many ways.

It is theoretically possible to do this to any humbucker, but practical problems exist, particularly with fully encased pick-ups. Where the entire pick-up is sealed in epoxy and the individual wire ends from the coils do not protrude, it is impossible. On a few pick-ups, the casing holds the whole thing together, for example, some of the Maxon pick-ups fitted to earlier Ibanez guitars. On some of the very cheap older Les Paul copies, it is quite likely that you may only find one coil in the casing

figure 10

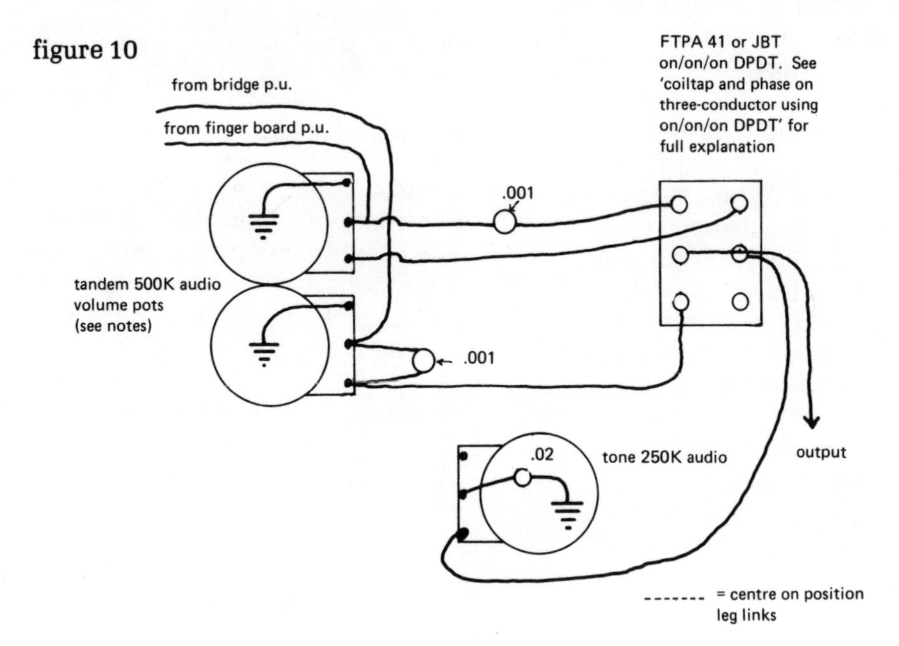

anyway, for example, Avon or Sakura. However, even where there is a decent pair of coils in the casing that will stand exposure, getting the casing off can be very difficult. I've seen casings that would slip off very easily simply by inserting a filling knife parallel with the internal side of the casing, and others that require very varied amounts of heat to break through a massive solder join. Great care is required if you are not to damage your coils, and a lot of heat could cause serious problems.

Most standard fitted humbuckers have a single conductor and shield, that is the hot wire with the signal, and the shield earthing the pick-up casing and the earth end of the coils together. If it is already open top, or you can get the casing off simply, adding an extra wire to the coils link is no problem. This extra wire need not run through the shield where you are going to use earth type taps, but if you are going to use one of the options that leave the first coil open circuit and take signal from the second coil via the tap wire, then shielding is essential to avoid extra noise in your sound.

Because of the difficulties involved in and the possible damage to an encased pick-up, it may well be best to consider selling the original if it is a 'name' pick-up, and replacing it with a more suitable custom unit.

For these reasons, the following diagrams relate to a converted two conductor custom open pick-up such as a DiMarzio Super Distortion or PAF. There must be many players who bought the simpler format pick-up who now feel that an extra option would be useful.

However, if you still want to tap an original pick-up, the following switching systems apply equally if you call your existing hot wire 'white', and your tap wire 'black'. Equally, of course, an extra tap wire can be added to a two conductor if you require a phase reverse facility as well as tap. See section on Schecter and Lawrence three conductors for switch options in the latter case.

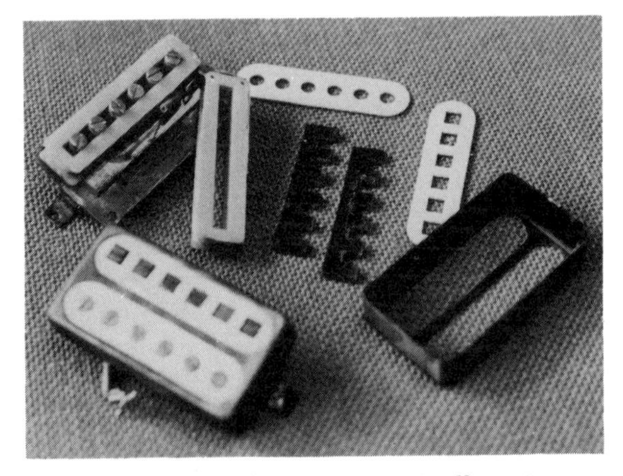

A pair of Maxon slot tops — actually quite easy to open. The conductors lie between the plastic-cased coils.

Pick-ups taken from an Avon.

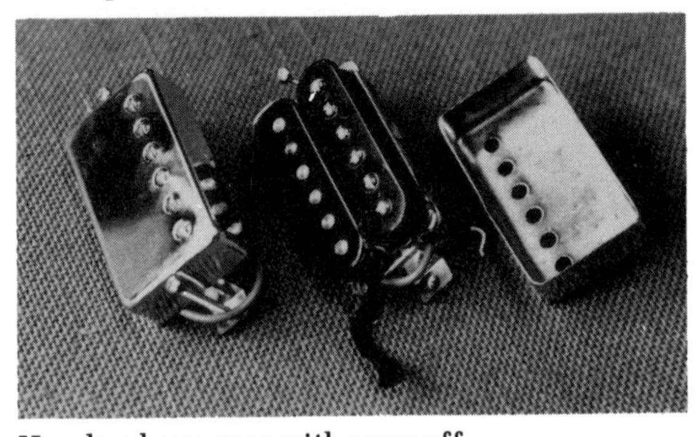

Humbuckers, one with case off.

At its simplest then, it can be done on a two conductor and shield humbucker. Most replacement two conductor and shield jobs are wired for phase reverse (whole pick-up) and they can be rewired for coil tap using the existing wires. The covering tape must be peeled back carefully to expose the links and avoid damaging the coils. First establish which of the two output wires you are going to use as hot to tie in the required phase with your other pick-up (you'll no longer be able to reverse phase on this tapped pick-up).

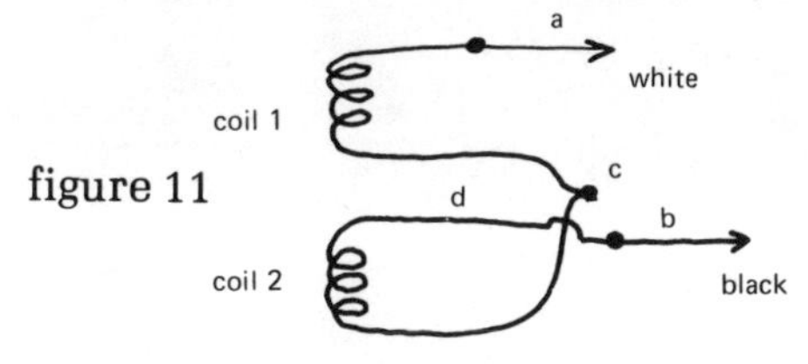

figure 11

Here, the phase is correct using wire *a* (white) as output and *b* (black) as earth. Remove conductor wire *b* from wire *d* in diagram above, and remove the little piece of tape binding covering joined wires at *c*.

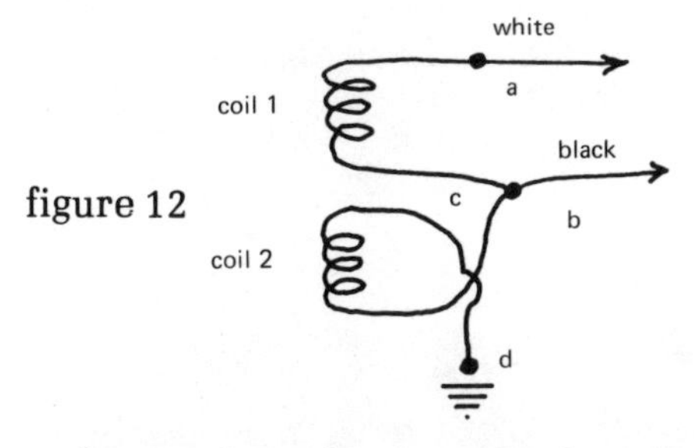

figure 12

Connect conductor wire *b* to joined wires *c* and tape up. Connect wire *d* to pick-up base, where it will earth via the shield in the cable. Carefully tape all exposed wire, and re-tape pick-up. Wire *b*, the black, is now the tap wire, and has to run to a switch or pot somewhere. Now take the white to the volume pot input leg as usual, and run the black to the spare leg of the tone pot, as below. Black will remain the tapwire for the rest of this section.

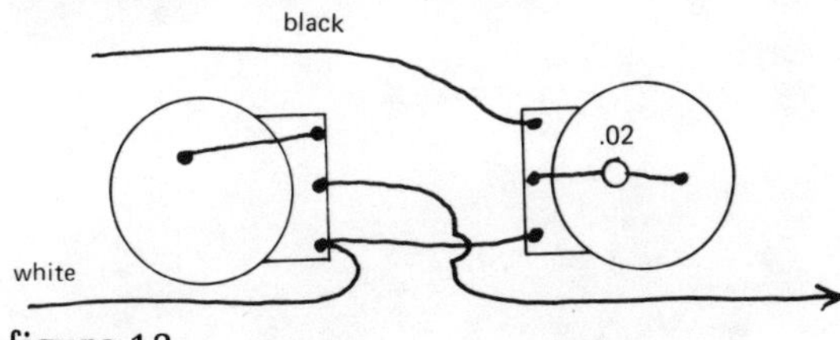

figure 13

The tone control will act normally from nought to nine, giving a normal full humbucking sound. From nine-ten however, if wired as in the diagram above, the treble frequencies of one coil (coil 2 here) will be cut off, giving the impression of a coil being switched off. If wired as below, nought-nine will be normal, but at ten the whole of coil 2 will be earthed this time, as the tap current is not going via the tone control capacitor.

figure 14

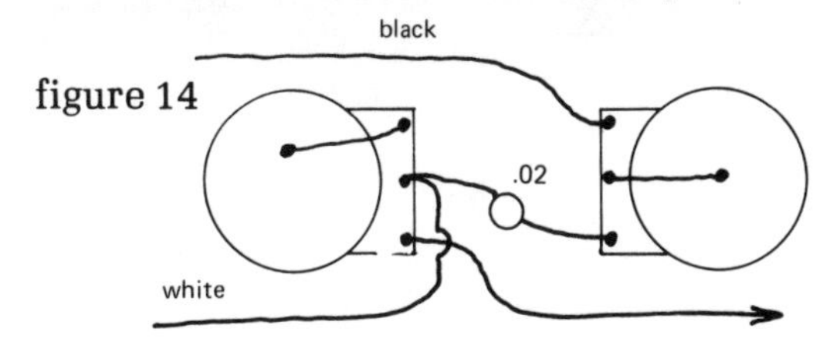

See 'Variable Tap — Partial / Complete' for fuller explanation of differences.

Alternative Tone Control Complete Tap

This one takes signal from the tap wire rather than earthing out one coil. When the tone control is from nought-nine, signal will be taken as normal from the hot wire, but as the tone control is moved up to ten, the earth for coil I will be cut off and there will be no circuit on it. Signal will instead be taken, via the tone control wiper, from coil 2 only. The capacitor does not affect the tap. The tone control works normally below nine.

figure 15

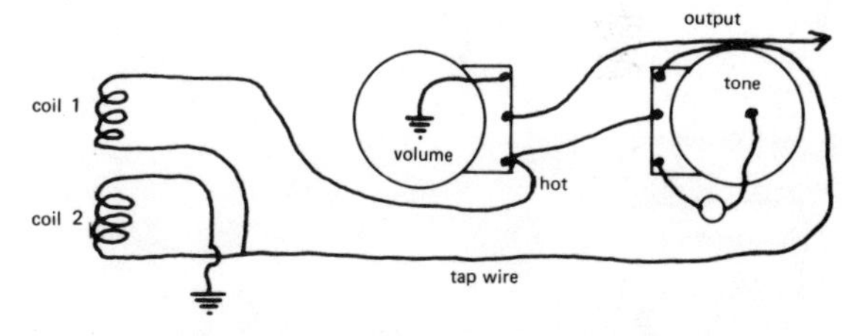

Switches can be used to operate coil taps. The white runs to the volume pot leg as usual, and the black is connected to the centre leg of a single pole double throw switch. One of the outside legs is connected to earth, either directly or via an .02 capacitor.
All these diagrams operate on coil 2.

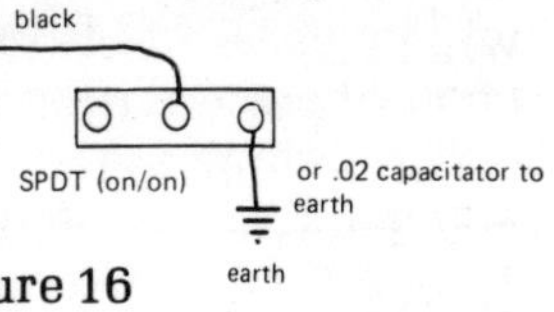

black
SPDT (on/on)
or .02 capacitator to earth
earth

figure 16

Alternatively, a DPDT can be used to operate simultaneous coil taps on two pick-ups at once, both pick-ups' white wires going to the positive side of the guitar circuit.

figure 17

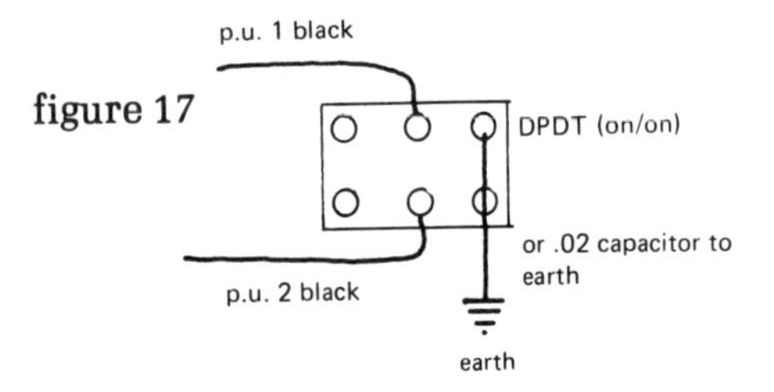

This would be useful where the guitar doesn't have separate tone controls. A tone control that is common to more than one pick-up can still be used to operate a coil tap, but only on one of the pick-ups. The DPDT can also be used to operate a coil tap on two pick-ups alternately.

figure 18

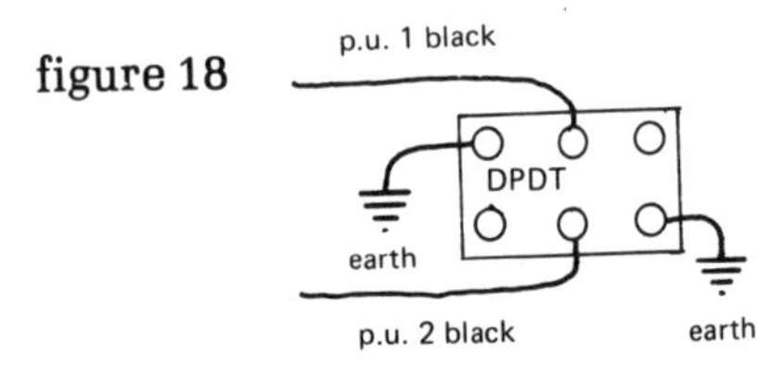

There is another way of switching off a coil on the same pick-up wiring, and this one will switch off coil I instead of coil 2.

figure 19

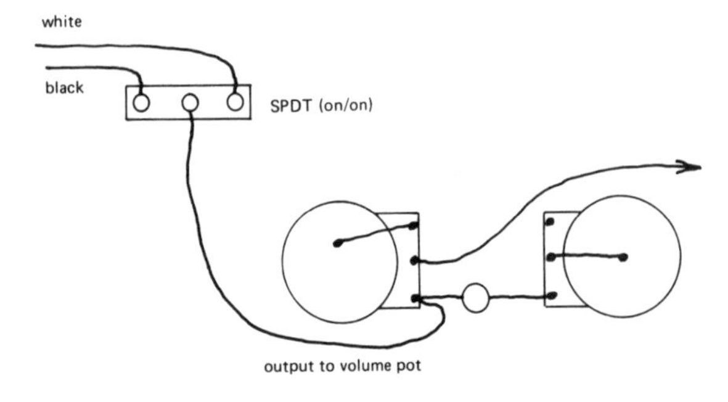

Here, when the switch is connecting to the right (white), the whole humbucker will be on — fed through to the volume control normal input leg. When the switch is connecting to the left (black) however, coil 2 only will sound, as there is no circuit on coil 1.

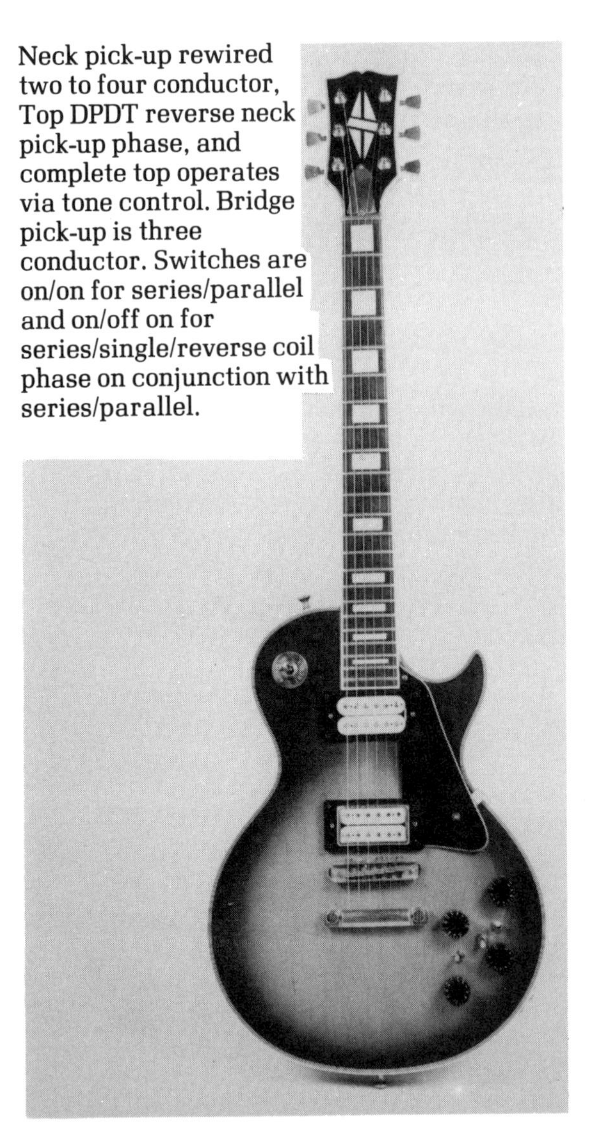

Neck pick-up rewired two to four conductor, Top DPDT reverse neck pick-up phase, and complete top operates via tone control. Bridge pick-up is three conductor. Switches are on/on for series/parallel and on/off on for series/single/reverse coil phase on conjunction with series/parallel.

The insides of the guitar after several experimental rewires.

Again, this tap can be done on two pick-ups at once on a DPDT, either simultaneously or alternately.

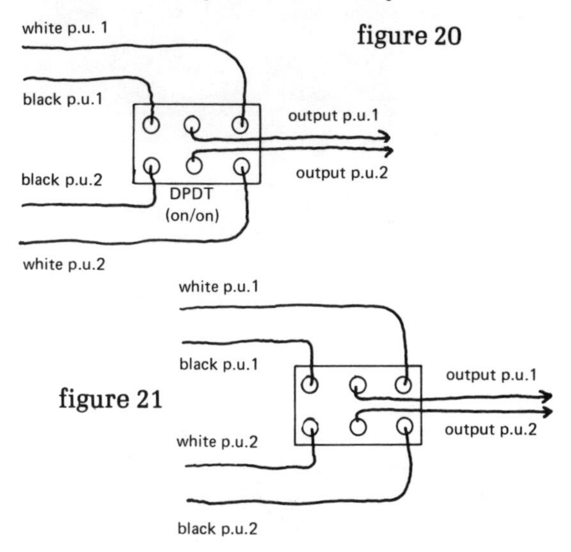

figure 20

figure 21

VARIABLE TAP — PARTIAL / COMPLETE

This is a simple set-up which will allow you to choose between a partial tap via an .02 capacitor, full humbucker, and complete earth tap. The main value of a .02 tap is that volume reduction is considerably less than with a complete tap. It is also tonally different. Some manufacturers claim that it retains the humbucking character of a pick-up. This is not wholly correct. The pick-up will not be humbucking for frequencies from the highest down to as far as the capacitor cuts. Below the point that the capacitor cuts to, it will be humcancelling. So, if you use an .01 as tap capacitor, the background noise you get will sound relatively shallow, if you use .05 as tap capacitor, it will be deeper, till, on a complete tap, the background noise will cover the entire frequency range that you can hear. Capacitors are pretty cheap items, and it is well worth experimenting with different values to find the best sound to suit you. This applies to tone controls as well, where personally, I currently compromise on depth of cut at .033.

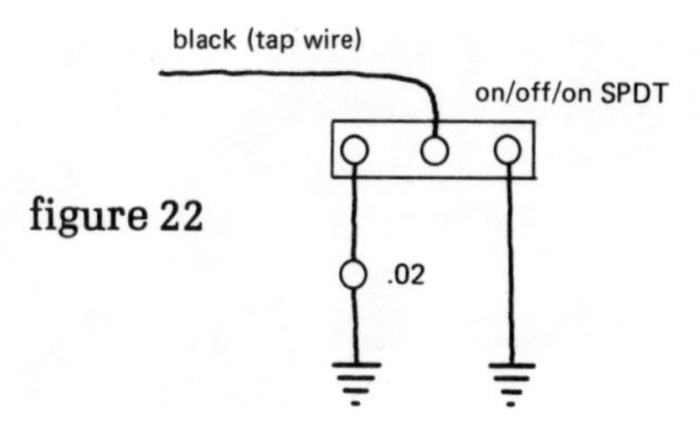

figure 22

While still on taps, there is a value in deciding which coil you want to turn off, as the tone will different depending on whereabouts the coil is centred on the string. For instance, in the bridge pick-up, the coil furthest from the bridge will generally give a throatier sound than the one nearer to the bridge. If the pick-up is further away from the bridge than usual, the forward coil will almost sound like a *"Fender" *"Stratocaster" guitar. Remember, if you've already wired up a particular tap, you can always change the affected coil position by simply turning the pick-up around, provided you have enough free wire. This has no effect on phase by the way.

Where you want the sound of the coil nearest the bridge, it may well be worth your while considering using parallel coils instead of a tap, as the harmonics that the pick-up is collecting from nearer the bridge will tend to dominate the tone anyway. If that is going to happen, then you might as well have the humcancelling properties of the parallel coils, which are still electrically out of phase. Personally, I find the sound of parallel coils too tight, and prefer the freer, more open sound of a single coil, but I do retain a switchable option for parallel coils on all pick-ups in case I get into a situation where hum becomes a problem. That I think, is the real value of parallel coils, the nearest thing to single coil tone with no hum. Anyway, we'll get to parallel wiring diagrams later on.

PICK-UP PHASE REVERSE ON A TWO CONDUCTOR

This is a very simple operation, and probably the most common modification

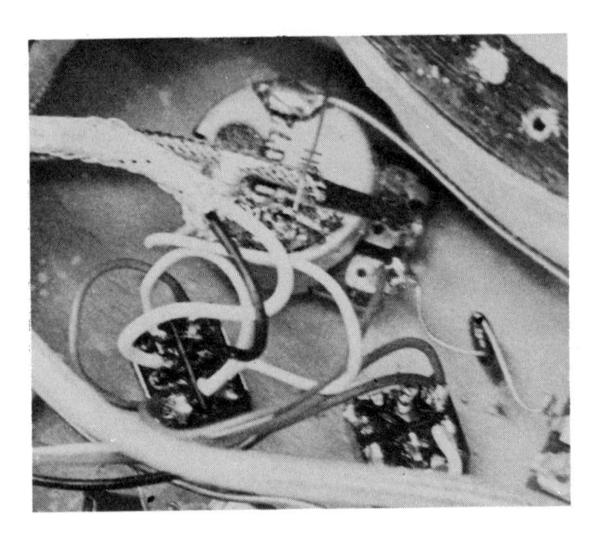

done to guitars. The fact that the pick-up is two conductor and shield, means that either end of the hooked up two coil system can be taken as hot, and the other linked to earth. It can only be done on an unmodified two conductor, (or four-more later) and a single conductor and shield will have to be rewired to two conductor for it to be achieved.

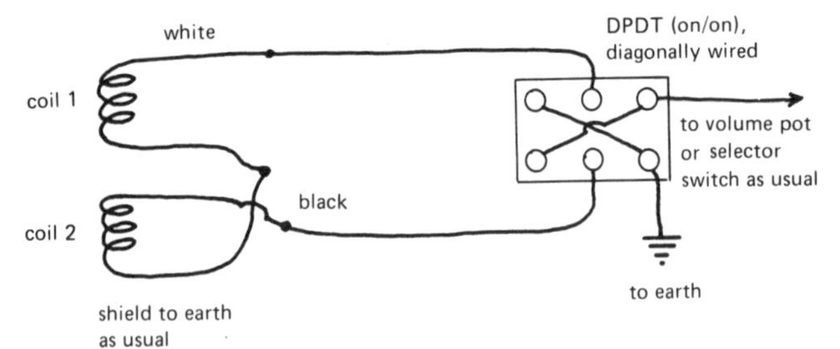

figure 23

THREE CONDUCTOR AND SHIELD HUMBUCKERS EXCEPT SCHECTER AND LAWRENCE

Some of the earlier replacement multi-conductor humbuckers available feature three wires coming out of the shield, and occasionally, three wires and a bare fourth, which last is used along with the shield for a slightly better earth connection. They are usually supplied with some directions for coil tapping or series parallel options. Turning the phase of the whole pick-up around 180 degrees in relation to another pick-up is not

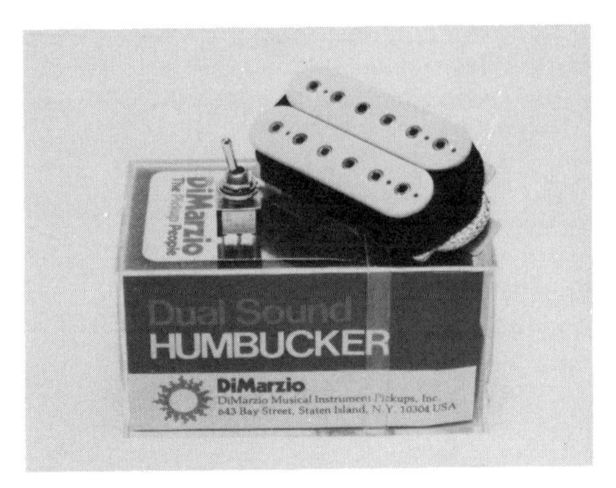

The original DiMarzio Dual Sound came three-conductor and shield supplied with an on/on DPDT for series/parallel or taps, whole pick-up phase reverse was not possible, and the pick-up was eventually changed to four-conductor and shield. The pick-up in the series mode, has the same characterisics as the Super Distortion.

A bolt-on neck Jap done up for demo with series/parallel on rear pick-up, and phase and tone control tap on rewired PAF.

possible, as the shield or bare wire would have to become the output wire in reverse phase. This just increases noise if it doesn't simply ground the whole pick-up. But there are still plenty of things that can be done with them, and all the coil tap control systems in the previous section apply if black and white leads shown here are wired together at the end and used in the same way as the black tap wire, and then the red here replaces the previous white. This is how the colours work out on most of them.

figure 26

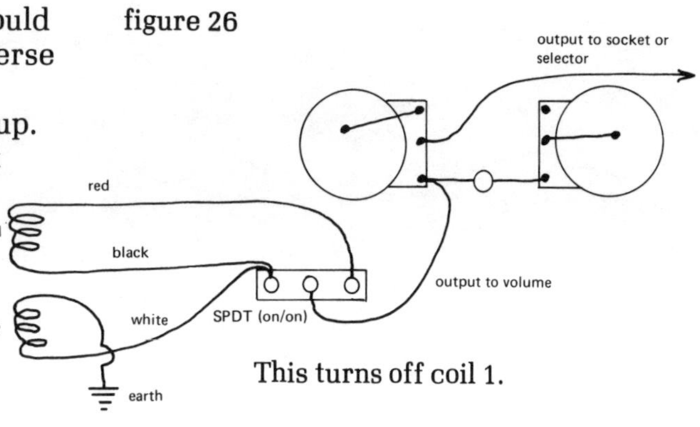

This turns off coil 1.

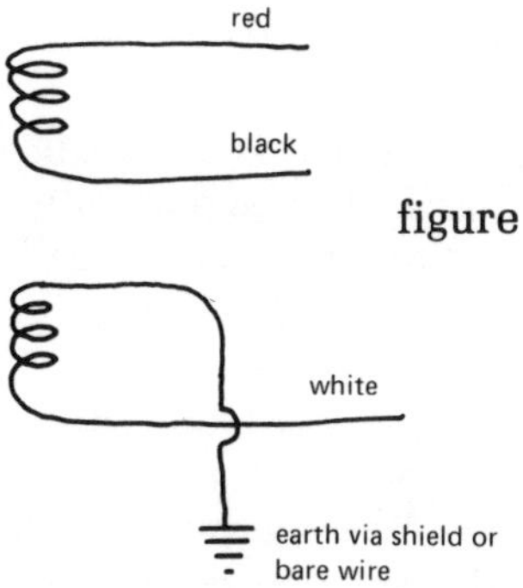

figure 24

Coil Phase Reverse on Three Conductor

What happens here is that the phase of coil 1 is turned around in relation to coil 2 and the other pick-up. The DPDT must have its corner legs wired to their diagonal opposites. The pick-up is still in series in either phase.

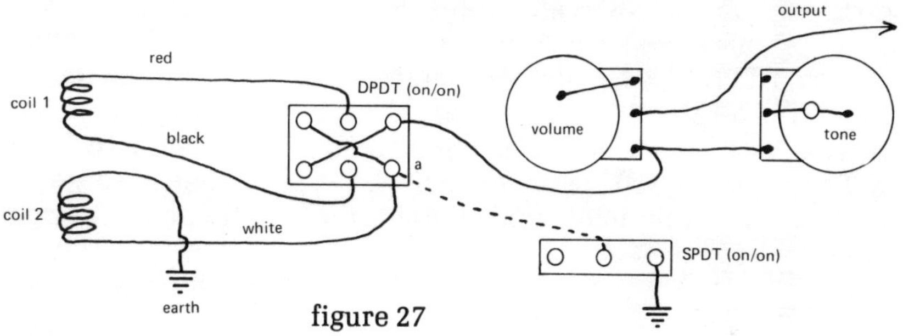

figure 27

Here's how two of the coil tap switch systems works out with a three conductor. This turns off coil 2.

figure 25

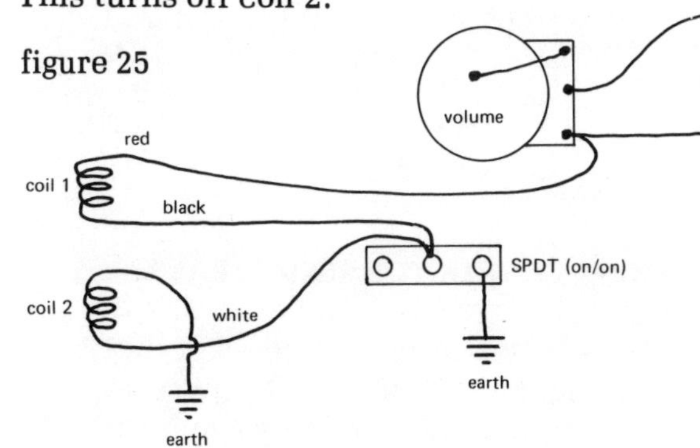

But by adding an earth type coil tap (dotted line indicates wire), coil 2 can be off altogether, and coil 1 used in either phase against another pick-up. The tone control tap can be used for this, but it should be the complete tap (centre leg of tone pot wired to earth and capacitor between volume and tone pots) not via the capacitor, as the remaining low frequencies from coil 2 will confuse the sound.

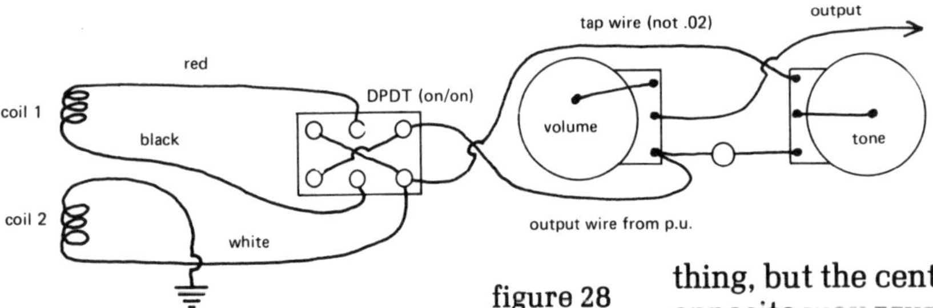

figure 28

Coil Tap and Phase on a Three Conductor using an On/On/On DPDT

This DPDT has a centre-on position as well as the side to side settings, and can be used to give series normal coil phase, single coil, and series reverse coil phase.

This one could cause you problems if you're unsure of the switch — it doesn't do centre-on both sides simultaneously. The first one I used was a Japanese switch, FTPA41, and this type of circuit is used in several production guitars. I have seen it in an Ibanez and in an Elektra.

This is the circuit I used for the FTPA41. The actual internal contacts first:

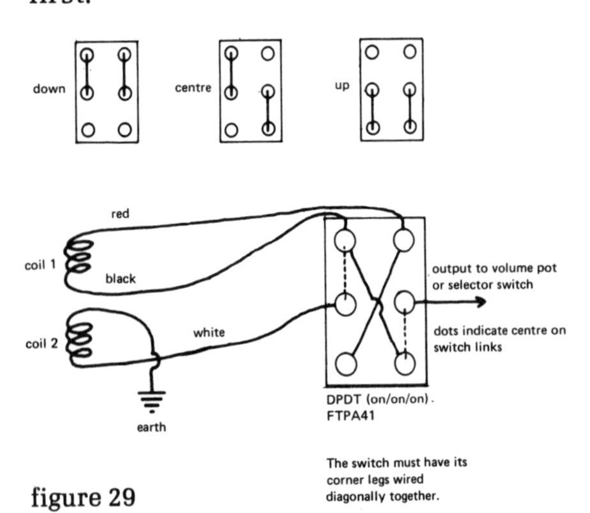

figure 29

In the centre position, there is no circuit on coil 1. Coil 2 only will sound.
The JBT centre on DPDT does the same thing, but the centre position is the opposite way round to the FTPA41.

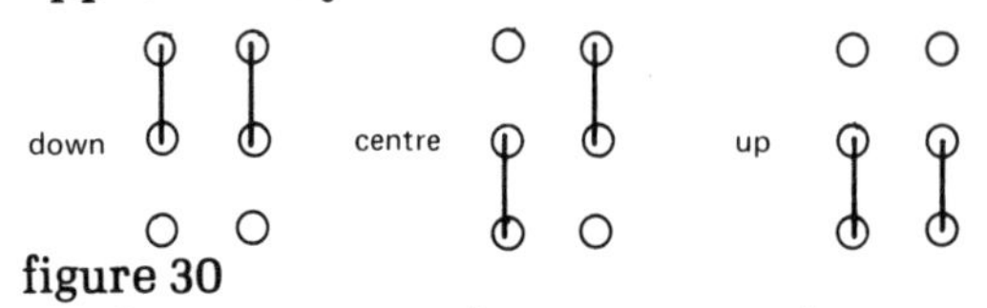

figure 30

The options, and wiring, are the same, except for series / single coil / parallel, see next section.

Reversing overall pick-up phase using either the JBT or the FTPA41 is possible where the pick-up is *four* conductor and is done by adding on an on/on DPDT, again diagonally wired. This will reverse the phase of the single coil as well, but will not determine which coil is tapped as other four conductor phase switches will — but see four conductor section for that. It will determine which coil will be out of phase with the other pick-up in a mix when reverse coil phase is selected, and that can be important for the tone.

figure 31

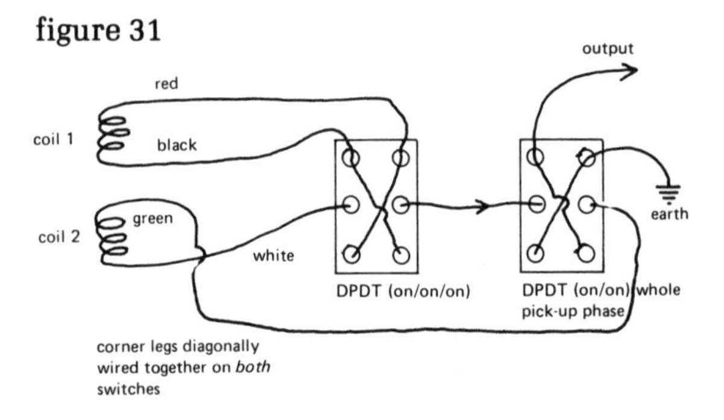

THREE CONDUCTOR SERIES / PARALLEL

Series is the normal humbucker, but running the coils in parallel gives a sharper edged sound, very similar to single coil, but picking-up from two areas of string instead of just the one. There are enough tonal differences, albeit subtle, to make it worthwhile considering a tap option as well. The dotted line and the switch in the brackets in each version indicate how it would be added, and the tone control tap could be used as well. The main advantage of the parallel setting is that it gives a sharp sound *and* cuts mains hum as it is still essentially operating as a double coil pick-up.

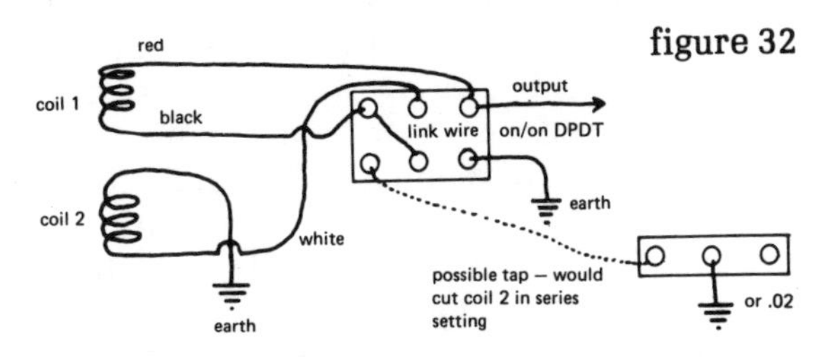

figure 32

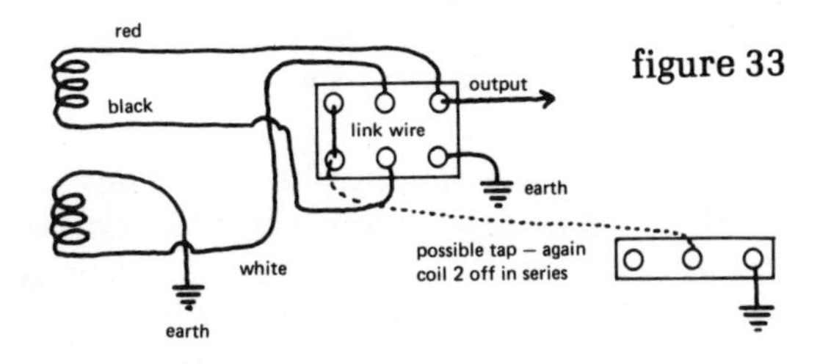

figure 33

Coil Phase Reverse with Series / Parallel, Three Conductor

Coil phase reverse is possible in conjunction with series / parallel, and would operate on coil 1, in series or parallel. The coil tap could also be used, operating on coil 2 as before, and giving the option of coil 1 on its own in an either phase mix with another pick-up. If you're going to add the two switches, the best tap control would probably be the tone control.

There is an alternative tap available here. If you use an *on/off/on* DPDT for the coil phase, the centre-off position will *cut coil 1*, and give you coil 2 solo when the series / parallel switch is set to parallel. I have this set-up on one of my guitars and find it quite useful. If you're considering both tap options, and they are possible together, life could get complicated mid-gig, and maybe using all this would be better to liven-up a single pick-up guitar.

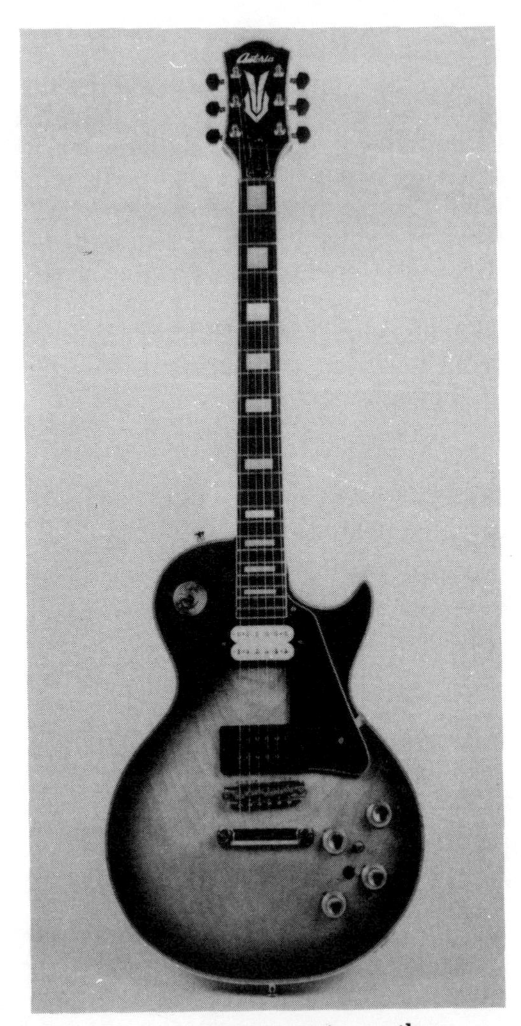

The same guitar as on page 30 in another incarnation. This time it has Tri sound type wiring series/single/reverse coil phase on rear pick-up.

figure 34

DPDT, either on/on, or on/off/on for coil 1 tap in parallel
red
coil 1
black
coil 2
white
output
earth
DPDT on/on series parallel
earth
possible coil 2 tap to tone control – operates in series setting

It is also possible, in even more complicated circumstances, to use an on/off/on DPDT for the series / parallel switch. In the off position, nothing will come out except a very light leak, which would be 'pre-ampable' if noise levels weren't so high in proportion to the leak. It does however, provide a simple means of cutting this pick-up off from its controls, and I have used this facility in order to route a completely different pick-up through those controls on its own.

SERIES / SINGLE COIL / PARALLEL USING ON/ON/ON DPDT

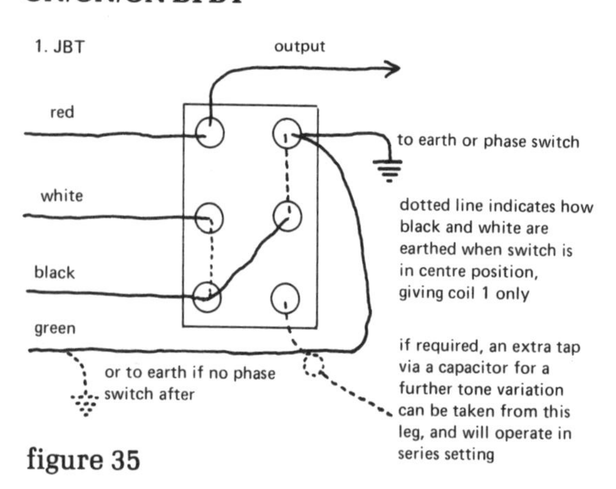

figure 35

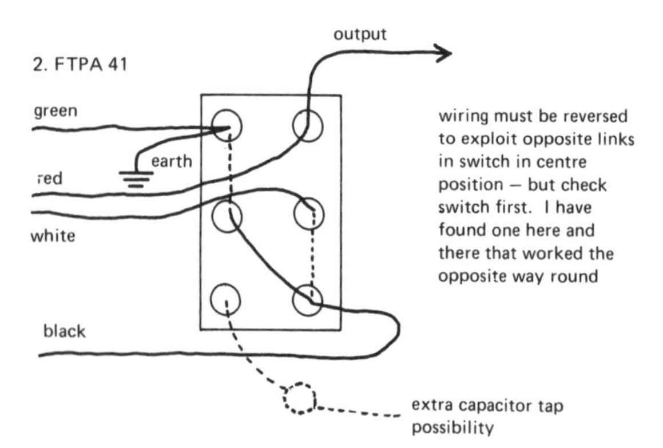

figure 36

PICK-UP MODE SWITCH

This is an on/on/on four pole double throw switch, which is more or less the same as two JBT or FTPA41 switches stuck together with one toggle. The beauty of it is that control layout on the guitar can be simple, yet very versatile. It will give simultaneous series / single / parallel settings on both pick-ups, and I have used it with a capacitor tap on one pick-up, run from either leg *d* or *e* depending on which pick-up I want to tap to the spare leg of the tone control. I can then say of the guitar from an operational point of view that I have a humbucker mode (series) with a partial tap on the tone control, or a single coil mode, or, where hum is a problem, a parallel mode. The partial tap has no effect on the single or parallel settings. With two tone controls, you can obviously have two partial taps, one for each pick-up, if you so desire, though I would tend to think of this switch as belonging in a simple one volume, one tone and one pick-up selector situation.

If a four conductor pick-up is used, the green from pick-up I can be run to leg *a*, green from pick-up 2 to leg *b*. They can be earthed separately, and *b* and *c* run on to a whole pick-up phase switch. It is not essential for them to go to the switch legs if phase reverse is not required, they can be taken to earth at any point.

figure 37

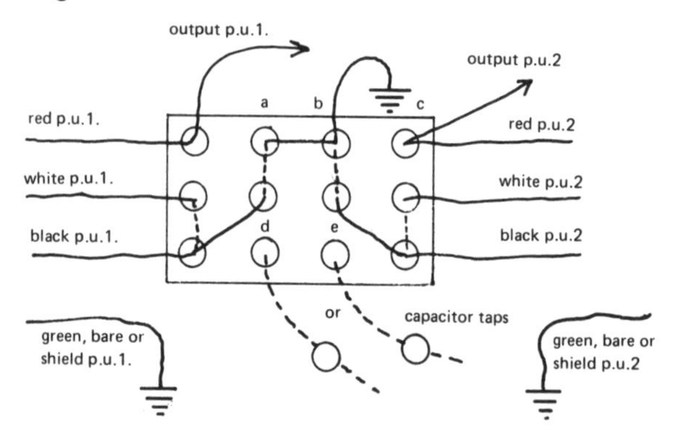

SCHECTER OR LAWRENCE THREE CONDUCTOR HUMBUCKERS

These pick-ups' leads are connected differently, and are designed to give a simultaneous coil tap and pick-up phase reverse facility. Series / parallel is not possible here without rewiring. The leads correspond to this arrangement in my diagrams.

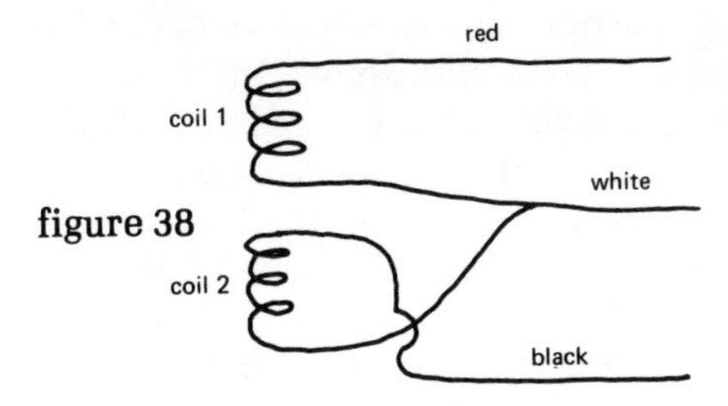

figure 38

Here, red or black can be taken as hot and the other as earth, depending on the phase required, and *white alone* is the tap wire which can be connected using any of the tap switch systems shown in the book except the ones that are in conjunction with a series / parallel and / or coil phase reverse. If the signal is swapped from red to white, and black run, *together with red* to earth, then the pick-up will give parallel, but in *reverse coil phase.* It is far better, if reverse coil phase is required, to go for it with a series option, as in parallel it may well be too thin and weak to be a lot of use even in a mix. I have found that parallel and reverse coil phase together have reduced the output of a three pick-up mix overall, giving only a minimal worthwhile tonal benefit.

oil tap and pick-up phase example on Schecter/Lawrence three conductor. Example 1

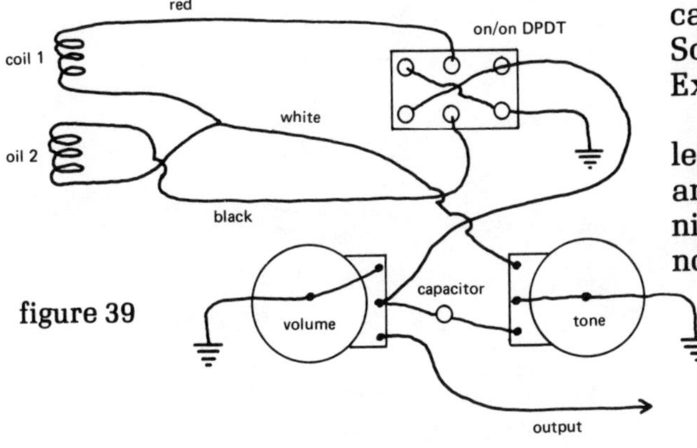

figure 39

If series / parallel and coil phase reverse options are required, then the linked contacts on the base of the pick-up in the case of the Schecter must be separated, and the pick-up rewired four conductor, or the existing cable can be used to rewire three conductor and shield where shield is pick-up earth. This would mean changing black from earth to the opposite end of coil I to red, and using white as coil 2 output and shield as coil 2 earth. Then all previous diagrams on three conductors would apply.

The Lawrence is sealed in epoxy and cannot be rewired.

Schecter / Lawrence three conductor. Example 1

In this 'earth type' tone control spare leg tap, coil 2 will be cut in normal phase and coil 1 in reverse pick-up phase, from nine-ten on the tone. Below nine will be normal humbucker.

Schecter/Lawrence three conductor coil tap. Example 2

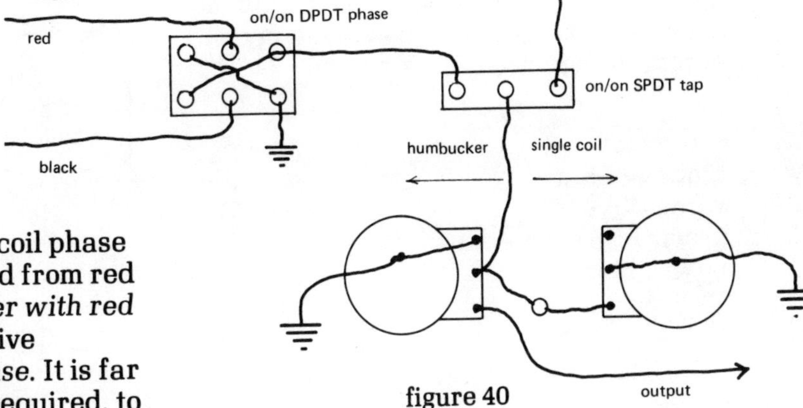

figure 40

Example 2

Here in normal phase, coil 1 would be (tapped) off, as taking the current from the white gives a 'no-circuit' on coil 1. In reverse phase, coil 2 would be (tapped) off for the same reason, as black would be hot or no circuit according to SPDT setting.
The pick-up base looks like this on a Schecter.

figure 41

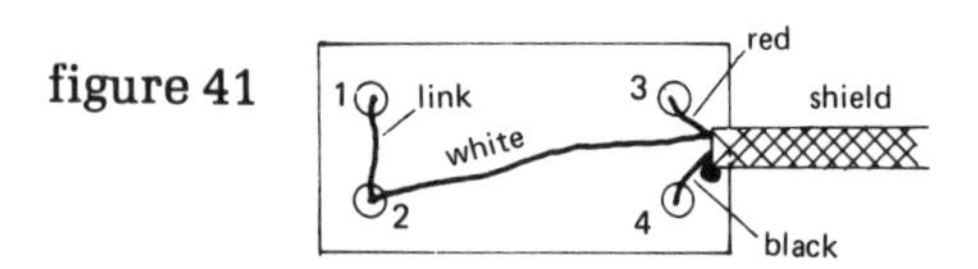

Rewiring a Schecter Humbucker to Four Conductor

To rewire to three conductor for series / parallel options, remove link between contacts one and two. Remove black from four and reconnect to contact one. Connect contact four to shield contact five along with shield. All three conductor and shield wirings shown in previous section then apply.

For four conductor and shield wiring, which I have used very successfully on a Superock, red goes to three, green to four, white to two and black to one. Shield goes to five as before.

This pick-up is very easy to rewire without fear of damaging the coils, as the contacts are clearly exposed on the base and easy to work on.

You may not necessarily be able to get four conductor and shield cable in these colours, in which case you must relate the colours you do get to the colours in my diagrams right from the start, for example:

red = red
black = blue
white = yellow
green = green — substitutes on a cable use.

FOUR CONDUCTOR AND SHIELD HUMBUCKERS

Now all the options are open, as the earth is no longer tied to the shield, but comes out on a covered green wire so that whole pick-up phase can be reversed as well. Naturally, if the green is run straight to earth, or connected to the shield, all the previously covered three conductor (except Schecter / Lawrence) possibilities apply in exactly the same way — coil taps, series / parallel, coil phase and so on.

Here's the wiring, again, if your colours don't tie in, carefully expose the coils (not the actual windings, just take off the cover or outer tape) have a good look and relate your colours to the ones shown here.

figure 42

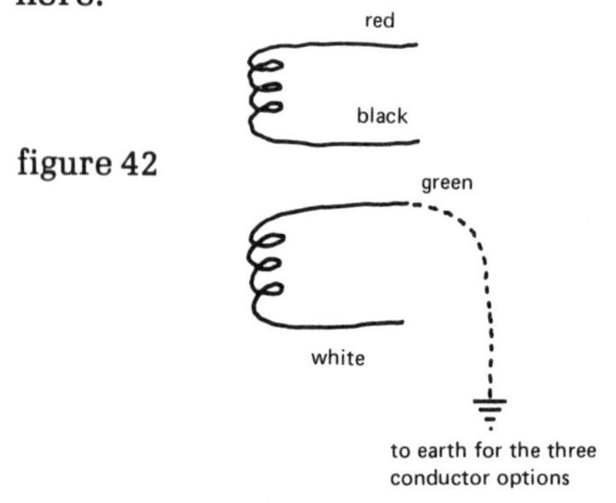

This is series / parallel feeding into the whole pick-up phase. Look at where the green is wired, and when you realise that, in reverse phase, it actually becomes the output, you'll see why it wasn't possible before.

figure 43

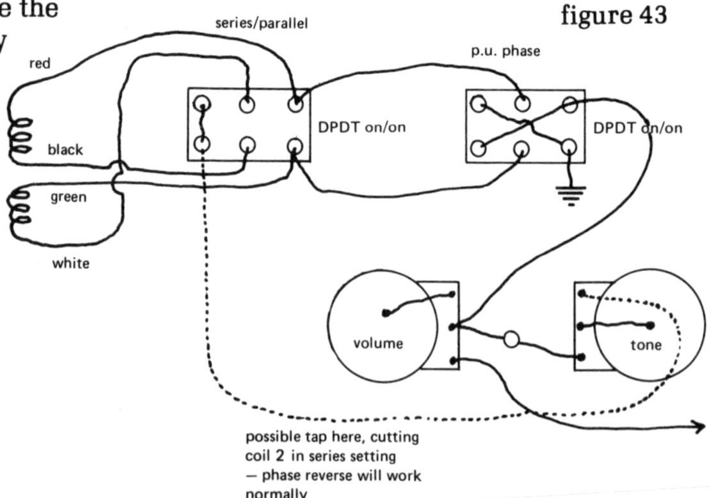

Four Conductor and Shield Humbuckers separate Coil Switches

Now the ultimate control on a four conductor (figure 44). Each coil feeds to a separate on/off/on DPDT, diagonally wired for phase, so that it is possible to feed either coil, together or one at a time, in either phase, to the series/parallel on/on DPDT. Single coil will not work unless the series/parallel is set to parallel, obviously, as in the series setting, there isn't another coil for it to be in series with. With both coils on, in either phase, series or parallel can be selected as needed. Whole pick-up phase is unnecessary, as both coils' phase can be turned around together, in or out with the other pick-up. The difference in sound between each coil is fairly subtle solo, and shows up more dramatically in mix with another pick-up, particularly in reverse phase settings, where more or less weight can be brought into the overall sound. I have found that this can make the difference between having a usable out of phase pick-up's tone or not. There are horses for courses, and this gives you the choice. You don't need an extra cut off point here in the series/parallel switch, as both coils can be turned off on the on/off/on switches. Exactly the same wiring applies to a guitar with two single coil pick-ups, where the series setting gives a strong thick tone with a useful little extra power.

Four Conductor and Shield Humbucker Taps with Phase

These are four conductor coil taps in conjunction with whole pick-up phase. Either full series humbucker or single coil will operate in either phase.
This tap cuts coil 1 in one phase, coil 2 in the other, as the earth reference in the tap changes from green to red according to phase — output will come from either white or black, depending on whether red or green completes the circuit to earth (figure 45).

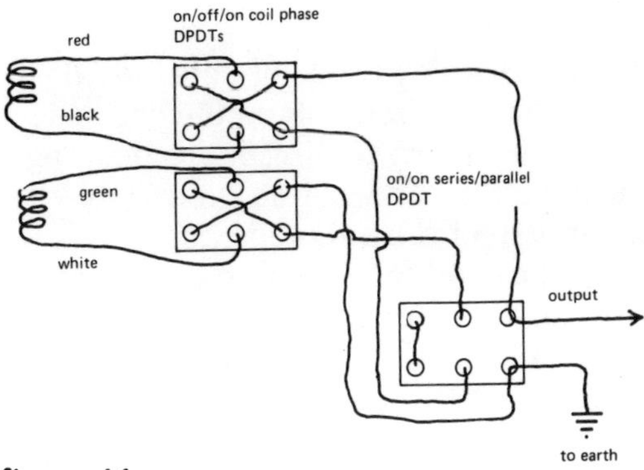

figure 44

figure 45

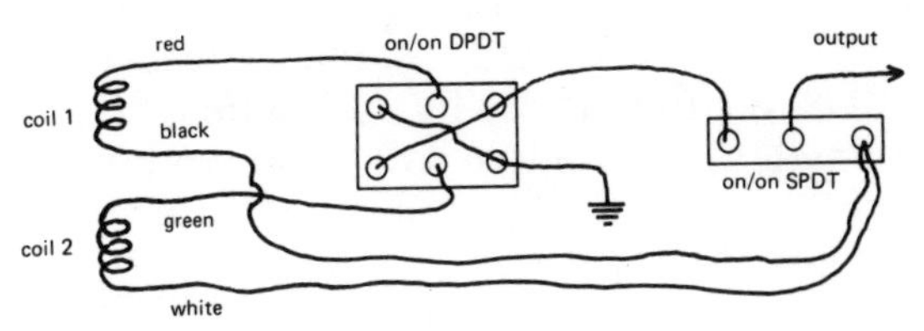

These two taps work in either phase, the opposite way round to the last one (figure 46). Instead of output coming from the central black or white wire, the earth reference for whichever coil is fed to the output on the phase will be on the corresponding output black or white wire. The whole of the other coil will be earthed.

figure 46

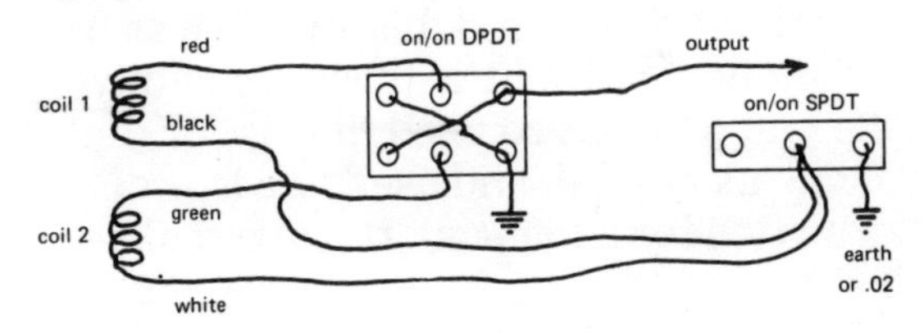

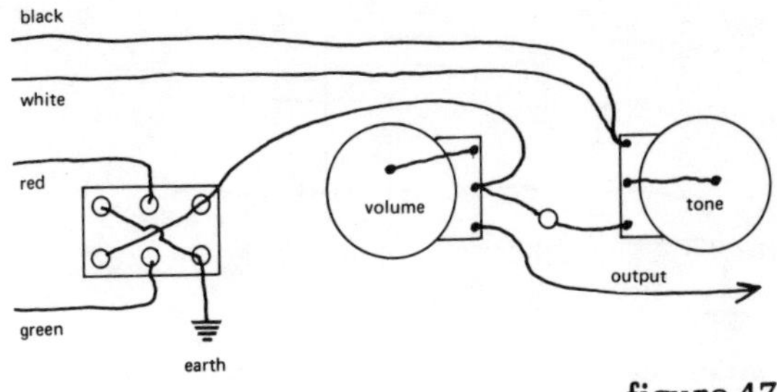

figure 47

Push-pull Pots

The Allen-Bradley range of pots includes a 500k with a switch unit on the bottom that is operated by pulling out or pushing in the pot shaft. The switch is entirely independent of the pot, and can, if desired, be used for something completely separate. This unit must be particularly useful to the player who wants extra switching capability, but doesn't want the extra switches cluttering up the guitar.

The top pot section operates normally, though it is much smaller widthways than usual.

The lower switch unit contains four on/off switches, operating in pairs. When the pot shaft is pulled out, the bottom two will be on and the top two off, when pushed in, the top two will be on, and the bottom two off.

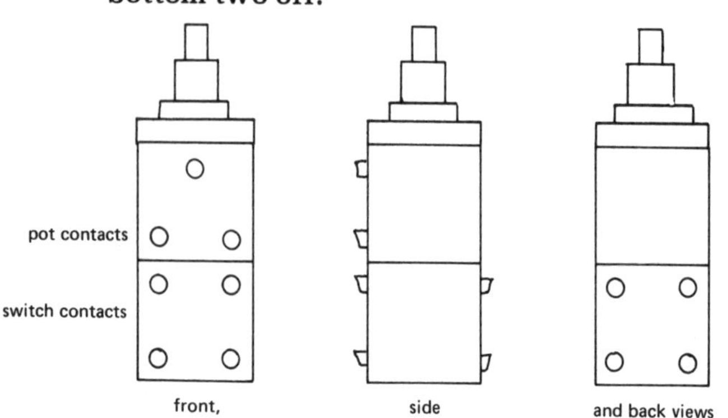

figure 48

The first time I used this switch was in conjunction with a little three-way active tone unit on a bass. I used the top for volume as normal, and used two legs of the switch for a tone-cut. It worked like this:

figure 49

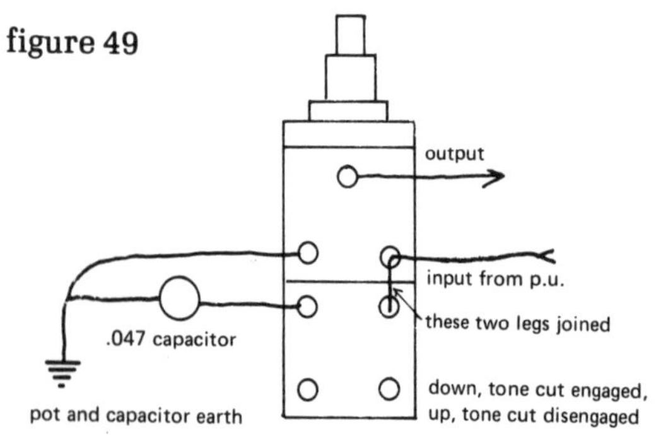

This switch can be used for whole pick-up phase, like this on a two conductor. I've drawn three sides, flat, so the wiring is clearer.

figure 50

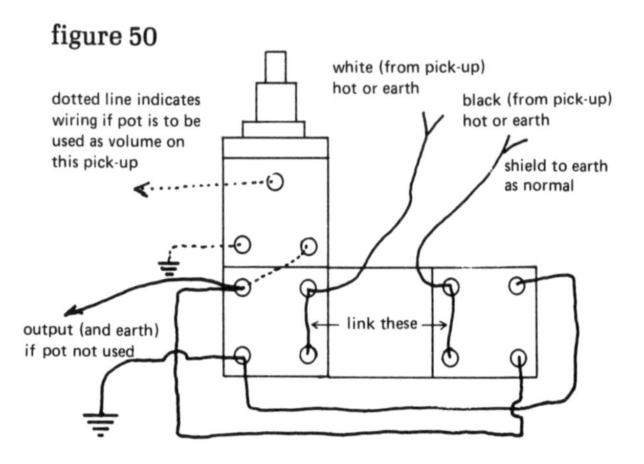

figure 51

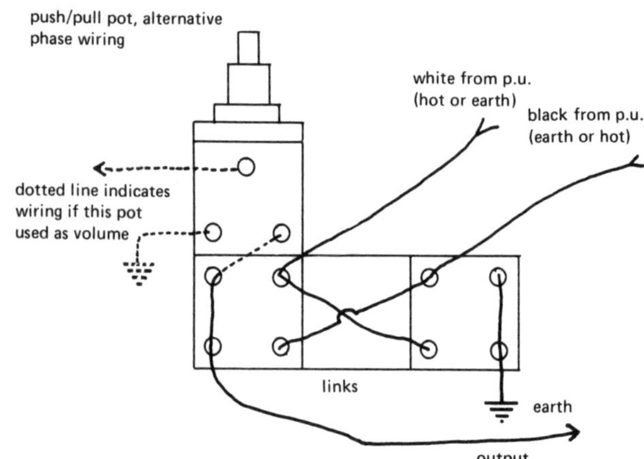

Here is how you would wire a coil tap on this switch, using the pot as volume.

figure 52

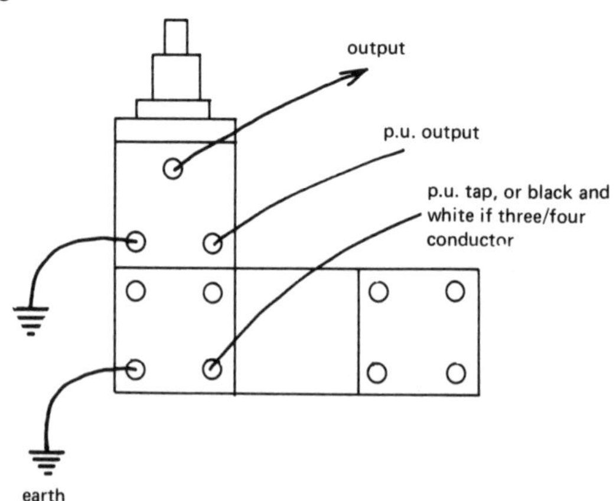

The coil tap would operate when the switch was pulled out, down would be normal. You can see this leaves a lot of switch unused, and if desired, the other side could be used for a tap on another pick-up, to operate either simultaneously, or alternately if wired on the top legs.

This one is series/parallel.

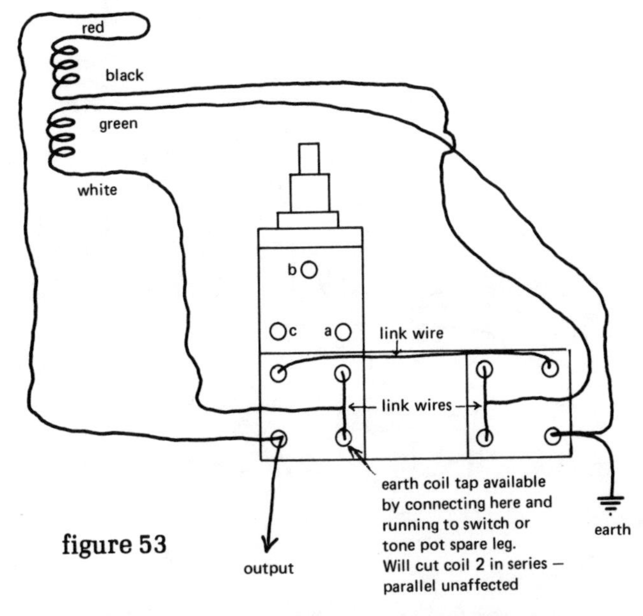

figure 53

If the pot were to be used as volume on this pick-up, output from the switch would run to leg *a*, *b* would be output and *c* would be earthed.

figure 54 alternative series/parallel

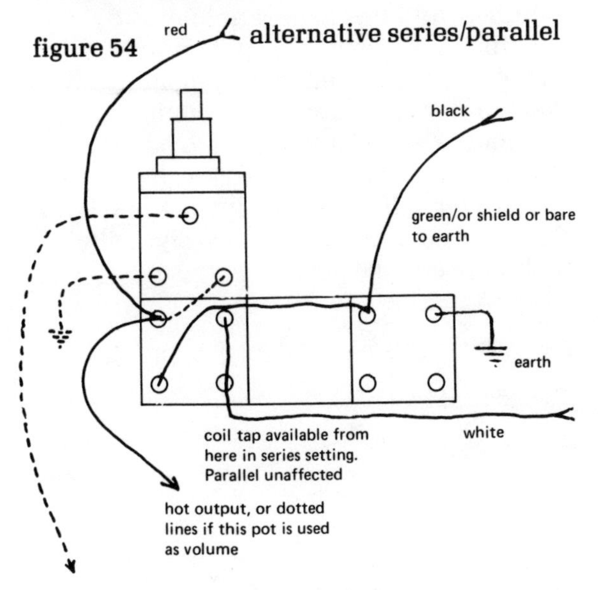

STRAT AND TELE WIRINGS

There are many replacement parts available for *"Fender" *"Stratocaster" and *"Telecaster" guitars, including standard switches. There is a five-way available for the latter, which replaces the three way on older models. Normally, replacing these items would be a simple matter of noting and copying the original circuit. However, you may be converting back from a more exotic circuit, or maybe the guitar has had an accident or fault. There are also a couple of little ways that the standard circuit can be altered — extra earthing, or possibly phase switching.

Here are diagrams of the ways to wire these guitars for standard performance, and otherwise:

How a *"Fender" *"Telecaster" guitar should be wired

The switch wiring here (figure 55) is simpler than the *"Fender" *"Stratocaster" guitar. If phase is to be added, it will have to go in on the neck pick-up before the black (earth) goes to earth on the back of the volume pot. It cannot go on the rear pick-up unless the plate under the pick-up is disconnected from the earth side of the pick-up wire. This plate is thought to contribute to noise, when it is intended to act as a string earth. It isn't terribly efficient. A better idea is to run a separate wire from the earth on the jack socket to underneath the screw on bridge assembly. You will also see that the only route for the earth generally to reach the jack socket is via the pot shafts and mounting plate. It is a good idea to link the backs of both pots with an extra piece of wire, this ensures a good soldered earth route. The .001 capacitor is standard fitting here, and helps give the guitar its characteristic tone.

This way of wiring the *"Fender" *"Telecaster" guitar (figure 56) is the same as the four conductor wiring I showed you a few pages ago. Here, the on/off/on DPDTs work on the separate

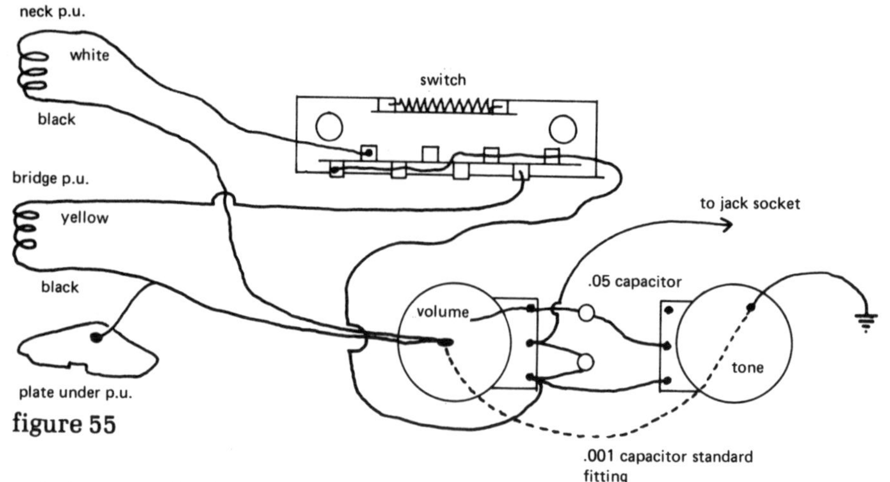

figure 55

coils in exactly the same way, it's just that the separate coils are actually separately positioned pick-ups. On the physical layout side, I have found that removing the three-way original switch, and drilling the three quarter inch holes for the DPDTs along the line of the old switch causes the minimum of disturbance, and is convenient to use. Relate the position of the switches to the position of the pick-ups to avoid on-stage confusion.

The string earth plate *must* be removed, and a separate string earth run to the underside of the bridge plate. Make sure the earth circuit is *complete.*

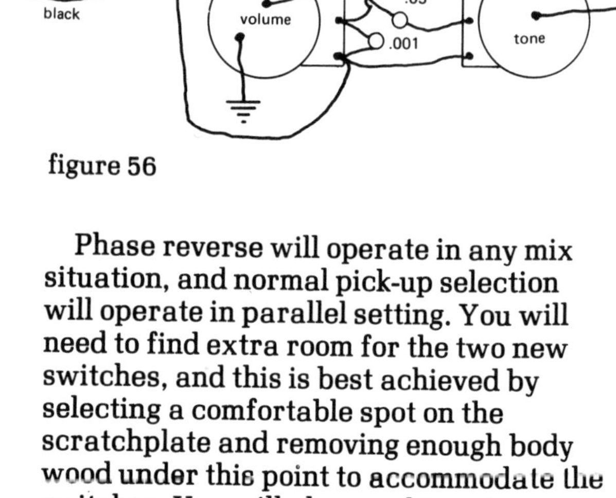

figure 56

This system (figure 57) gives you two extra switches for pick-up phase and pick-up series/parallel, and retains the original three-way selector. Series can be operated when either the front (neck) pick-up or both pick-ups are selected.

Phase reverse will operate in any mix situation, and normal pick-up selection will operate in parallel setting. You will need to find extra room for the two new switches, and this is best achieved by selecting a comfortable spot on the scratchplate and removing enough body wood under this point to accommodate the switches. You will also need to cut a shallow channel for the wiring. (see Notes) You will not get a signal when back pick-up is selected while series/parallel switch is set to series.

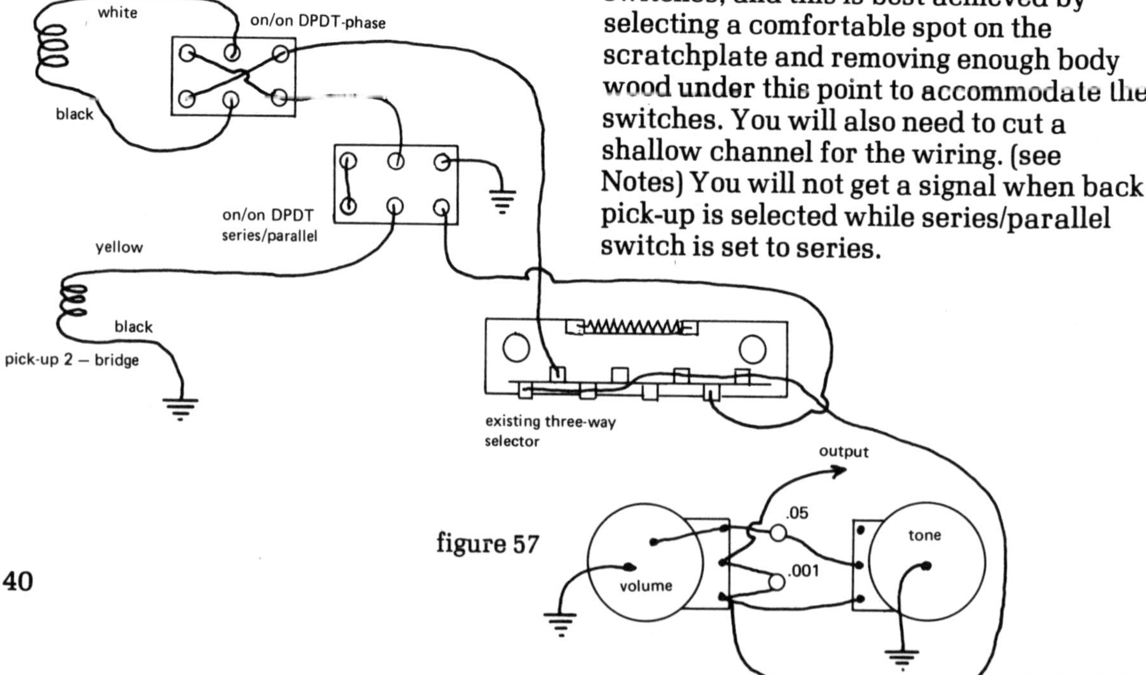

figure 57

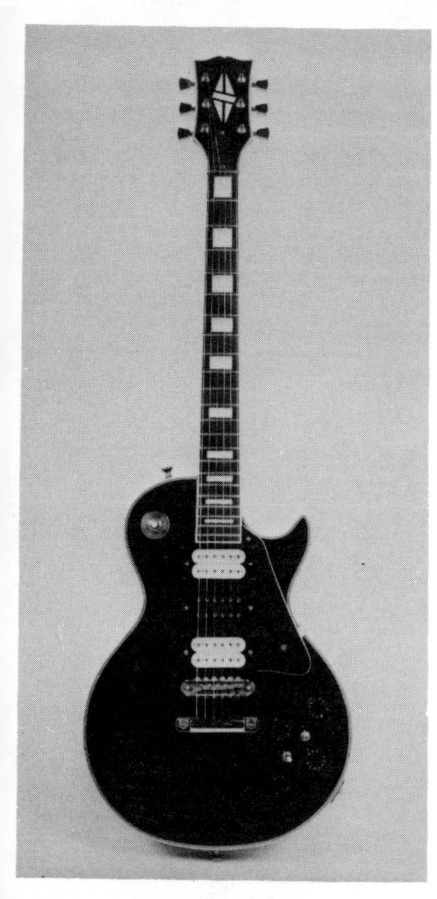

This Jap copy sounds quite Knopfler-ish courtesy of brass nut and bridge, coil taps, centre pick-up and .001s.

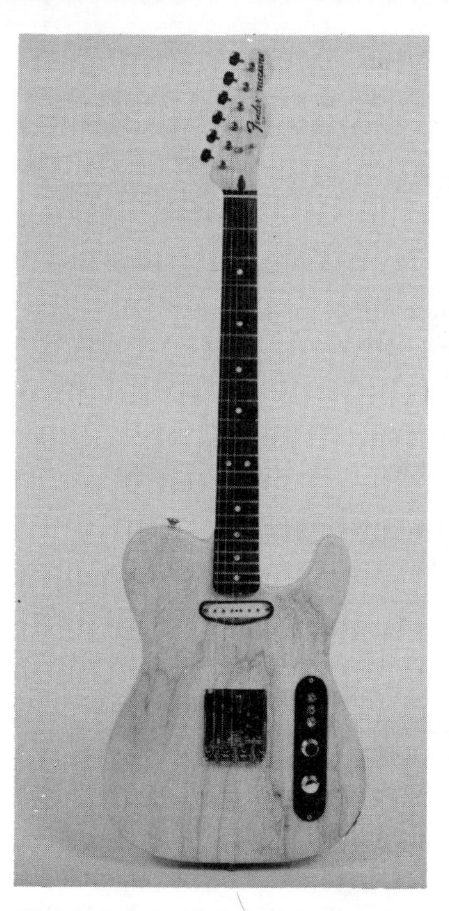

This *"Fender" *"Telecaster" guitar has off/on in either phase for each coil, plus series parallel for its pick-ups.

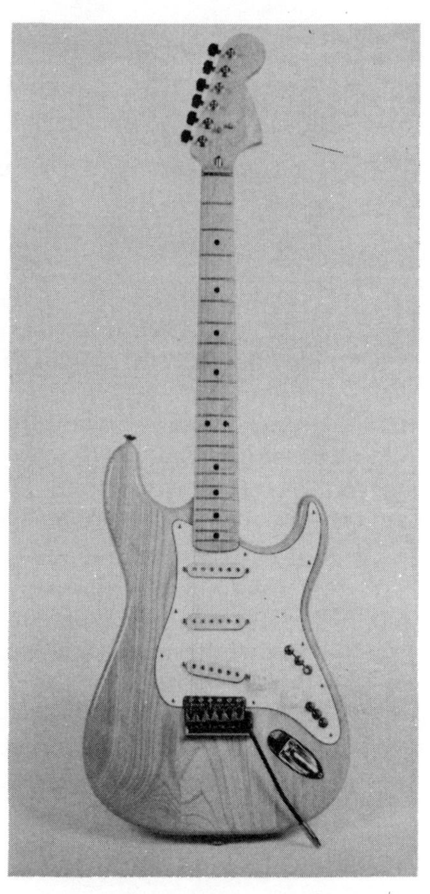

I use this guitar for testing pick-ups — the switches are three separate on/off and three phase in/outs master volume and tone.

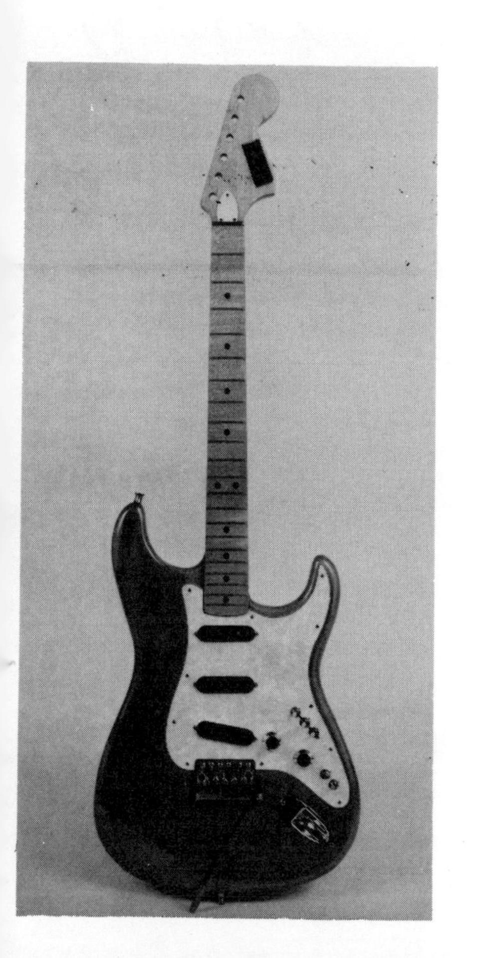

Left: This one, getting new machine heads at the time, is the same except that there are only two phase switches which are all that are necessary really.

Right: This is my test-bed Westbury, which has had just about everything wired in it at one time or another. It's ideal because the control compartment is so large.
Left: The guitar in more elegant days. Incidentally, these guitars are mainly maple, and will give a phenomenal sustain.

How a *"Fender" *"Stratocaster" guitar should be wired

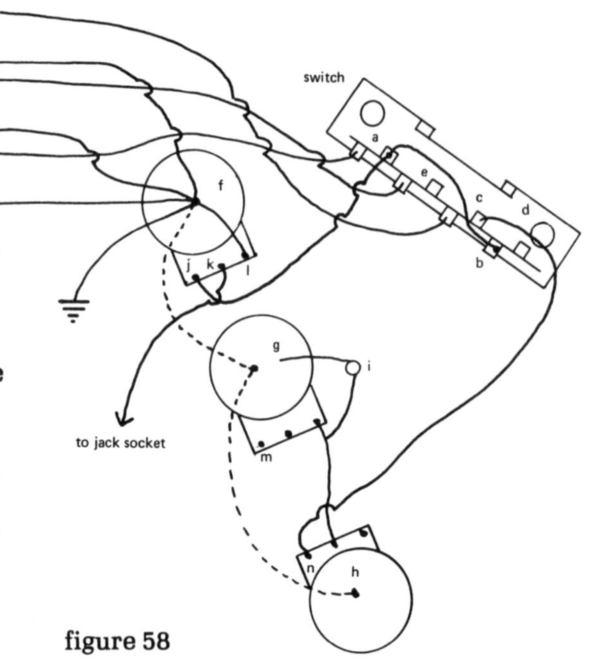

figure 58

The three black pick-up leads opposite all go to earth on the back of volume pot *f*. This earth point is also connected to volume pot leg 1. A suggested improvement is to continue the earth wire to tone pots *g* and *h*, which only earth through the foil shield. I have found a guitar with tone controls that didn't work because of this and *"Fender" *"Stratocaster" guitars are notorious for bad earthing. Leg *a* on the far side of the switch is connected to leg *b* on the opposite side. This is so that all pick-ups can be fed to the volume control. Point *b* inside the switch is in contact all the time. Point *c* is where the wire to the centre pick-up tone control comes off, and point *d* is the same for the fingerboard pick-up. The bridge has no tone control, but if desired, it could be run off point *e*. Points *j* and *k* are the in and out legs of the volume pot. If desired, an .001 capacitor could be added here. Phase switches would have to go in before the black pick-ups wires got to earth at point *f*. *i* is the capacitor which serves both tone controls. Tone control wires connect at *m* and *n*.

This is the simplest way of wiring a *"Fender" *"Stratocaster" guitar to get all the parallel in and out of phase combinations. The three DPDTs are on/off/on, and go in along the line of the old selector switch for minimum disturbance. Personally, in view of the fact the pick-up changes aren't so fast as the old selector, I would ditch one of the separate tone controls (possibly leaving the space for a powered output?) and use a master tone. That is shown here, but if you do want to use the separate tone controls, then how to wire them individually is on the next page. Don't forget to make sure the earth circuit is complete, if you're not earthing to shielding tape, run an extra wire between all the earth points and the earth on the output jack — the foil on many *"Fender" *"Stratocaster" guitar I have found is unreliably weak.

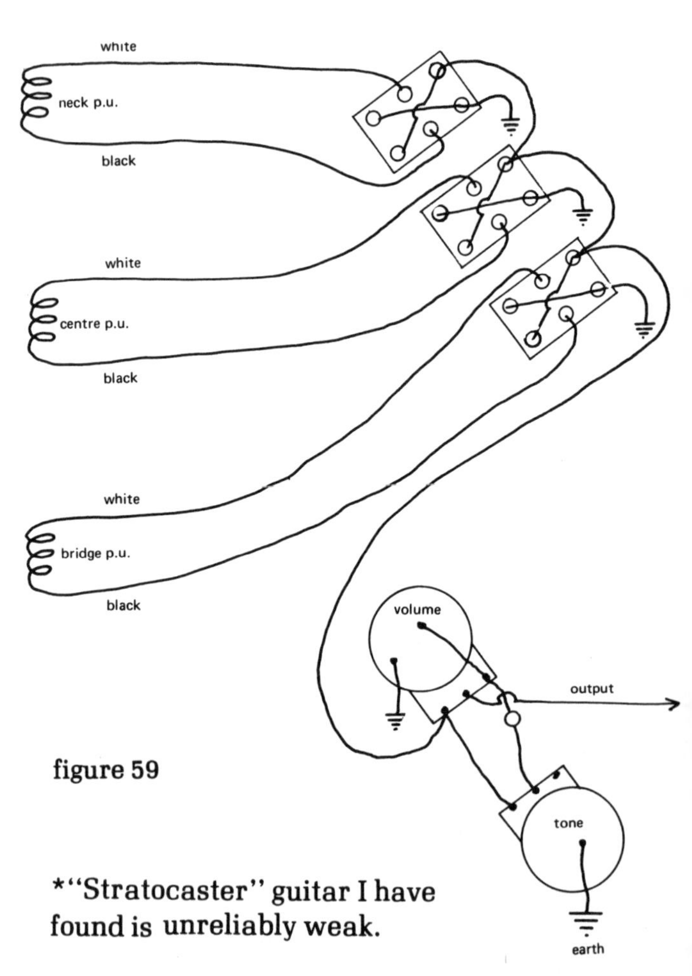

figure 59

This is how you wire an individual tone control. It must not go to earth at any point, or it will mess up the phase reverse.

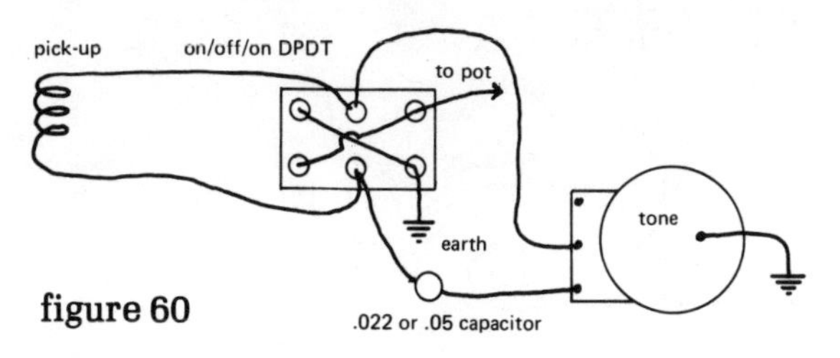

figure 60

It connects directly to the pick-up wire at the closest point to the pick-up, and here, that is on the same legs of the DPDT as the pick-up wires. If it goes anywhere else, it will affect another pick-up. The earth all gets taken care of at the output end of the on/off/on DPDT here.
When the pick-up is switched off, so is the tone control.
You should earth the pot casing as usual.

ON/OFF/ON S/DPDTs USE ELSEWHERE

I've already mentioned that an on/off/on can be used to cut off a pick-up's output. They can also be used to route a pick-up — I've done this on one of my own guitars, and found it very handy. The diagram on this page shows how an on/off/on SPDT is used to route a signal in with either of the other pick-ups. Bear in mind that although it is only a single coil shown here, this signal could equally well be coming out of any of the switches or combinations shown on the preceding pages (figure 61).

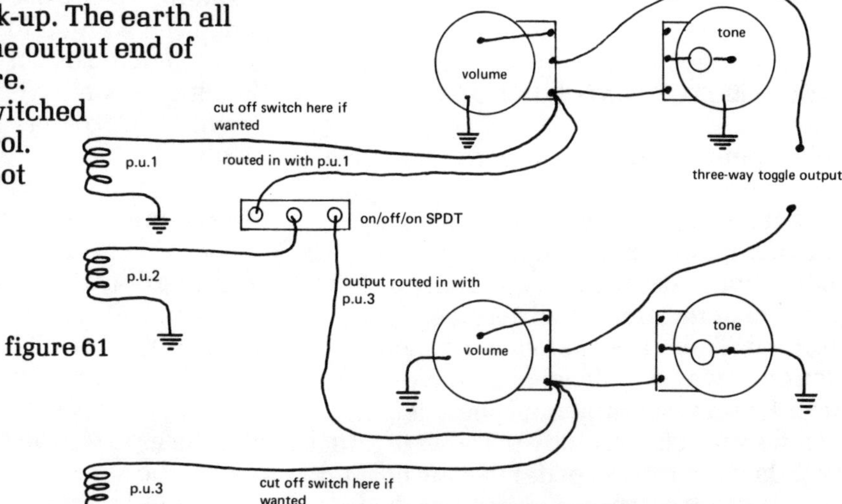

figure 61

Here, an on/off/on DPDT is used to route a centre pick-up in either phase, in either with the back pick-up, or, if a centre-off DPDT is used to cut the back pick-up output at the series/parallel switch, on its own. I have used this one

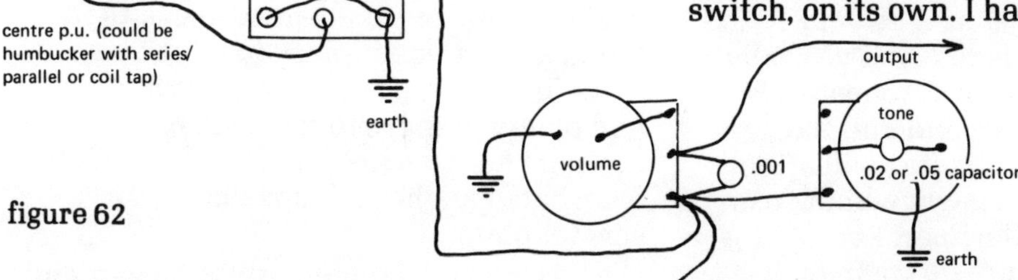

figure 62

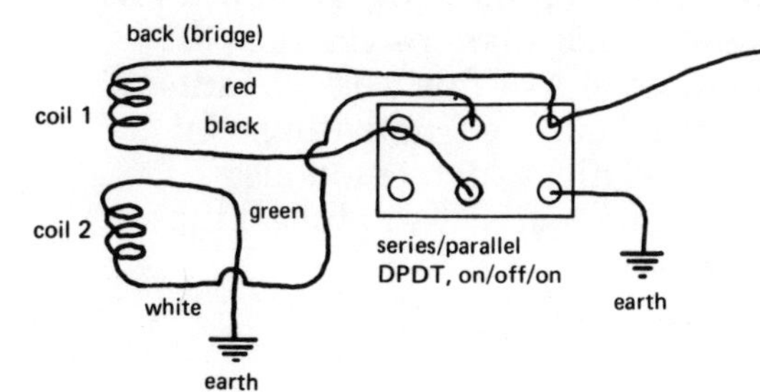

along with coil taps on several three pick-up guitars, and by using a very trebly centre pick-up, and and .001 across the volume pot, can get a very convincing 'out-of-phase' sound like a *"Fender" *"Stratocaster" guitar as well as the normal humbucker sounds (figure 62).

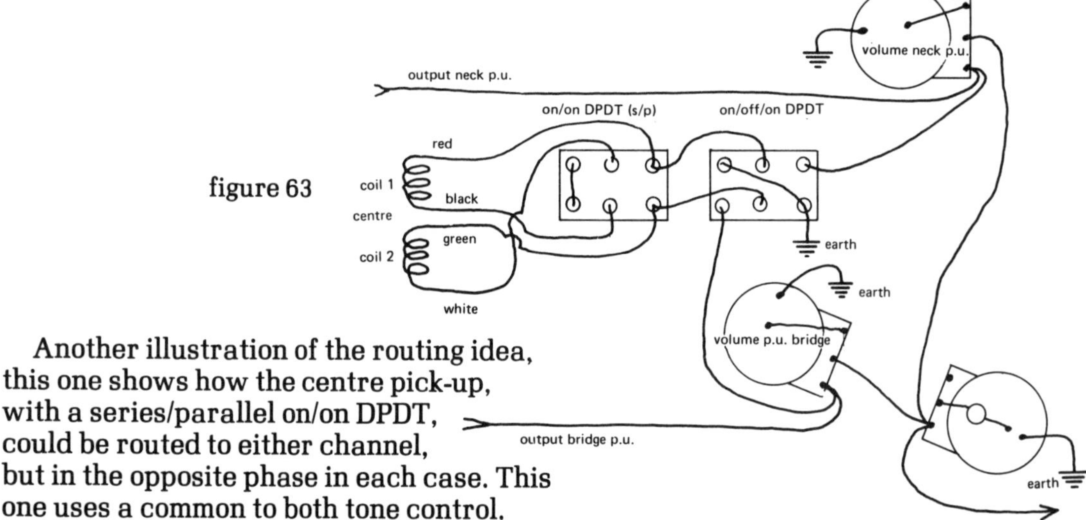

figure 63

Another illustration of the routing idea, this one shows how the centre pick-up, with a series/parallel on/on DPDT, could be routed to either channel, but in the opposite phase in each case. This one uses a common to both tone control.

If cut out switches are used on bridge and neck pick-ups, no selector toggle is necessary.

WIRING EFFECTS UNITS ON BOARD

Active pots are around, either active tone or power-boost pots, and are very simple to fit assuming you've got or can make the space. Manufacturers supply instructions, and mainly it's simply a question of tacking the wires on as directed. There are custom workshops around who will build you an active circuit, and this really is a specialist job.

However, it is perfectly possible to add the guts of an effects pedal to your normal passive electronics, assuming that the bits aren't too big. Most effects units now come with small printed circuits which take up very little space, so all you need is room for that, a battery, and one or two controls.

Another point that should be very seriously considered is that you've really got to like an effect to have it constantly available in your guitar, and that the effect output from your guitar will affect other effects units you might want to use from time to time on the floor. For instance, a compressor will completely change the results you get from an attack sensitive unit like an envelope filter, and a compressor on the floor will bring up any noise from a guitar mounted unit as the note decays.

In my mind anyway, there's only one unit that can be justified inside a guitar, assuming you've got all the passive tone range you want, and that is a pre-amp. Others will no doubt feel differently, and the illustration that follows will demonstrate at least the principles involved.

The example uses the guts of an MXR Micro-amp, which I have used with great success in several guitars. The current consumption of this particular unit is very low, and you can expect a battery life of up to 1500 hours. The pot controls the gain of the unit, so you do need to retain your existing passive volume controls, and the gain will go from unity, that is, output the same as what's going in, to around twenty times. It also lowers output impedance to 470 ohms, and cuts out treble loss on long leads. I have found that with most amps, it will go up nearly three quarters clean, and then the last few notches will distort beautifully. This varies according to the amp's sensitivity. It will also drive ordinary headphones.

As for space, on most of the guitars I had plenty to spare in the control compartment, on another, I took out wood from between the pick-ups under the scratchplate.

Make a note of input, output, power and switch connections before you take the effects unit to bits — this is important and will save you hours of frustrating trial and error bodging which could also overheat components. Don't forget the heatsinks.

You need to retain the unit's gain control, as it will be noisy if wired up without it flat out and overall volume controlled from guitar volume. There is a slight (under a second) delay when power comes on, hence the need for standby, but if you prefer, wires at *a* and *b* can be joined together and the switch cut out, then the unit will be power on all the time. In this case you only need an SPDT (or push-pull pot 1) for effect on or off. Connecting the earth of the power supply via a stereo jack socket, second positive and earth, means that power will be cut automatically when the jack is taken out regardless of switch setting (figure 64).

If you decide to retain the power switching capability, you may well find that you get a nasty little clunk coming through the amp as you switch the power on. This can usually be eliminated by connecting a 470k ohms resistor across contacts *a* & *b* on the switch on top of the power negative wires. This will allow enough leakage to ensure that capacitors are charged up and ready to go.

Outside Power

You may find youself in a position where you've mounted active or effects units in the guitar all right, but there's no way there's room for the battery — for example, there's not a lot of room in a standard *"Fender" *"Telecaster" guitar — or you think battery access is going to be too fiddly for easy changing. I've used a very simple device for powering from outside the guitar. Electrical parts suppliers have a simple, undrilled box with a screw on bottom plate that is similar to a small effects pedal box, or you can use an old effects box or a tobacco tin.

Connect the battery connectors to a mono jack socket, positive terminal to the jack socket tip connection, and earth to the screen connection, and mount in your box. When drilling for the jack socket, watch out for evil little razor sharp bits of swarf, and clear them up before you go any further. Make sure you avoid shorts by taping all contacts and the inside of the box (figure 65).

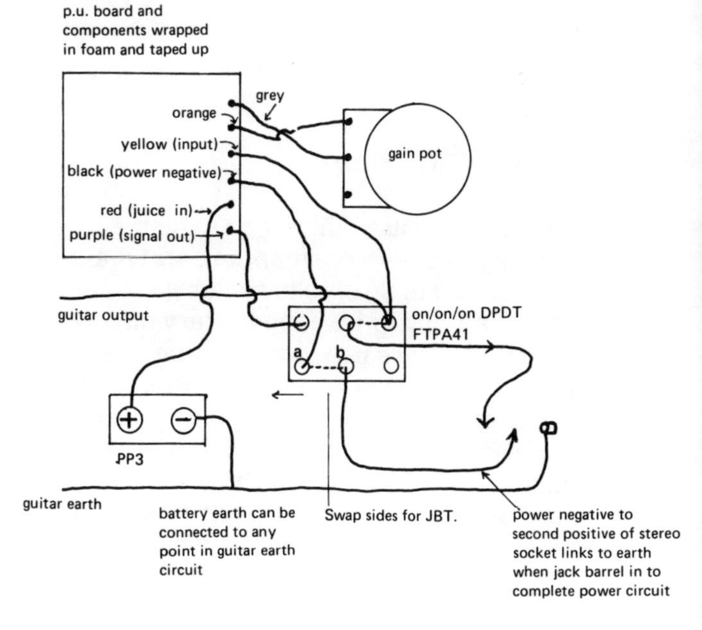

figure 64

In the guitar, put in a stereo socket in place of the mono socket, and taking the output of the guitar at the end of everything including powered unit(s), connect it to the tip, or first positive connection of the socket. Connect the earth to the screen connection as usual. Take the power leads from the unit, and connect the positive to the ring, or second positive of the jack socket, and connect the earth to the guitar earth. Using a stereo split lead, run the signal lead, first positive, to the amp, and the power lead, second positive, to the battery box to complete the battery circuit, and if you've wired up correctly, you should be in business. The earth is common to both parts of the lead.

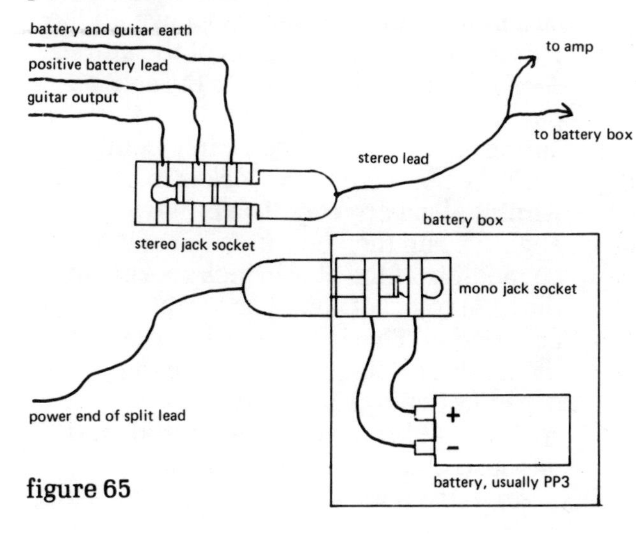

figure 65

Rechargeable Batteries

These make sense where you expect a fairly high power consumption, and it also makes sense to be able to recharge without having to take the battery out of the guitar. I have used units which are PP3 size, nickel cadmium, and which can be recharged from a companion charger over a seventeen hour period at nine milliamps for a full charge. The units deliver a nominal 8.4 volts, but in fact are capable of long term over-charging, and can be kept up at over nine volts. As most nine volt effects units will operate quite happily down as far as six volts, peak level is not a problem.

Charging onboard is fairly simple. Replace the battery connectors on the PP3 charger with a phono plug, connecting charger positive to phono male, and charger negative to phono shield or earth. Connect two wires to your in-guitar battery connector, running one from battery positive to phono socket female connection, and battery negative to phono socket shield or earth. The socket can then be mounted at a convenient point in the guitar. If the phono socket earth is going to come into contact with any part of the guitar earth, it will probably mess up your switching system and leave everything permanently on. If this is the case, or if you are mounting the phono socket onto the same plate as the guitar output jack, the answer is to move all the guitar earth from the earth of tho stereo socket used for switching to the second positive of the same socket. Thus the guitar earth will only come into contact with the plate when the jack is in and you want it all on anyway. The battery negative can then be run to the earth connection of the stereo jack socket via the phono socket shield or earth connection. This is the way it is done in the following diagram where high power consumption by LEDs makes a rechargeable battery an essential, and onboard charging very desirable.

An extra point about onboard charging is a handy one to remember, if you get caught out, as I did, with a low battery, it is possible to extend the charger lead and run the guitar on mains for the night. I didn't find any problem with noise in this situation, though I have been told that there is a possibility of it.

Check Lights

Here, the 4PDT is used to extend the basic off/standby/on pre-amp switching capability to include check lights. The check lights are Light Emitting Diodes, and each will need to be run in series with a resistor. Your electrical parts shop should be able to advise on a suitable value resistor for the type of LED that you purchase. The circuit shown here is complicated by the fact that the battery charge socket is mounted on the same plate as the jack sockets, so the whole of the guitar earth has to run to the middle stereo socket connection so that it is all off when the jack is withdrawn. This gives a light sequence of green = passive output/green and red = standby/ red = powered output. Because of the heavy power consumption of most LEDs a cut out switch is included on the positive side. Most LEDs are polarity sensitive, that is, they will only work in one current direction.

figure 66a

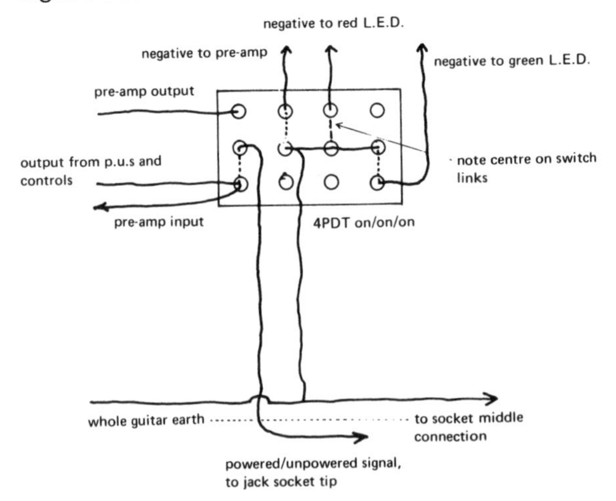

figure 66b

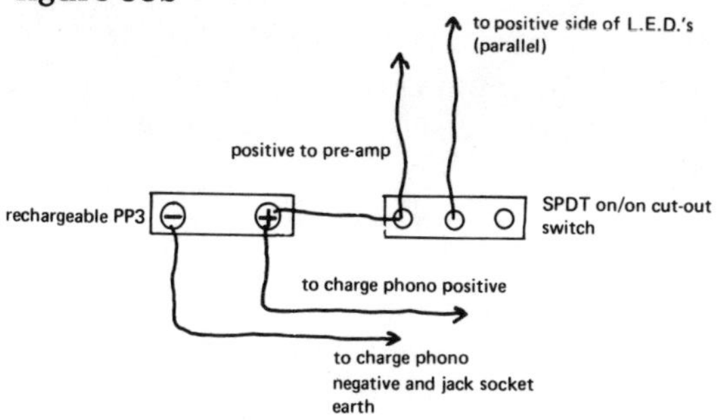

to positive side of L.E.D.'s (parallel)
positive to pre-amp
rechargeable PP3
SPDT on/on cut-out switch
to charge phono positive
to charge phono negative and jack socket earth

Single Check Light

A simpler version of this uses only one LED, though having a charge socket is still a good idea. The LED can be added using the original on/on/on DPDT, and runs in parallel with the pre-amp (or effect of course) from the same switch leg. The cut out switch can be added if desired — you don't have to use an SPDT, I do because it is easier to get toggles that are small enough and that match the rest of the switches. There are some nice push-button latching action switches around, indeed, it is possible to get DPDT and 4PDT push-button switches. These will only give on/on, obviously, and the normal objection to them, i.e., you can't tell by looking at them what the situation is, doesn't apply with a check light.

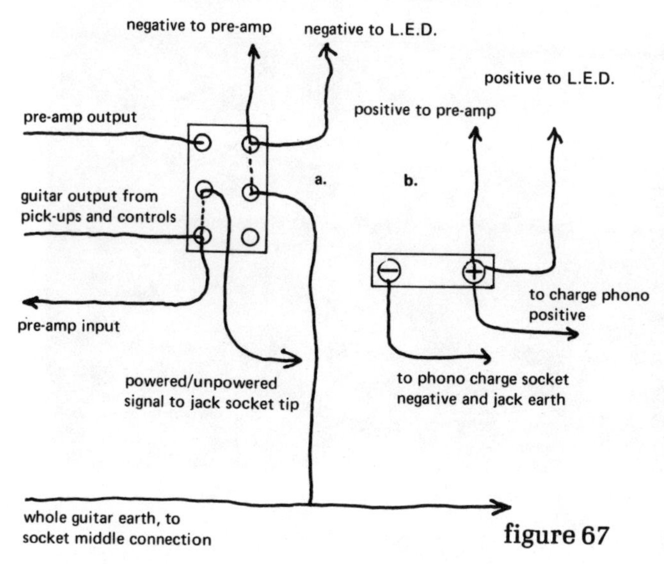

figure 67

Stereo

As used on most guitars, stereo wiring is fairly uncomplicated. The separation is merely between pick-ups as a rule, and can be achieved very easily. The output will consist of two signals and one common earth, so fingerboard and bridge pick-ups' signals must be kept separate right the way through the guitar.

Usually, there would be separate tone and volume controls for each pick-up, but it is possible to cut down to one overall volume and tone by using stereo pots. Simply, these are two pots stuck together and worked by one shaft. They are usually available in suitable values for guitar, 500k or 250k, and more rarely, 1 meg.

The pick-up selector switch needs to be a similar type to the JBT or FTPA41 centre on DPDT, and would wire up like this.

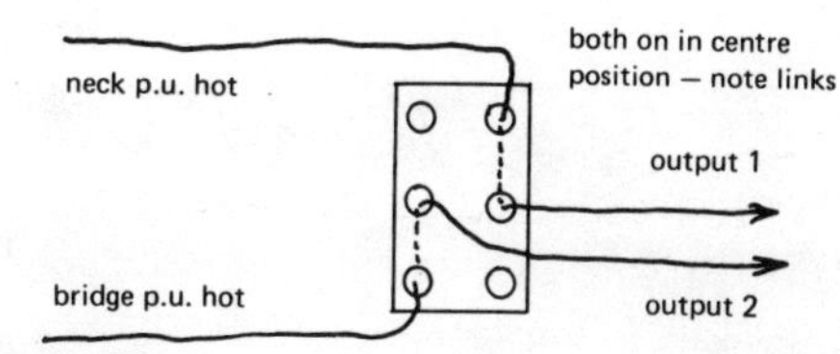

figure 68

You must check out the centre-on switch links first. Because the outputs from the switch stay separate, it can be wired in before or after the tone controls according to convenience. On a normal mono guitar, a simple on/on/on selector would have to be wired in after separate volume and tone controls, but before overall single volume and tone for obvious reasons. On guitars with separate volume and tone for each pick-up, the mono selector switch is usually the last stage before the jack socket.

Split Octaves Bass

This separation between the two pick-ups can provide some interesting and useful effects on bass when the pick-ups each

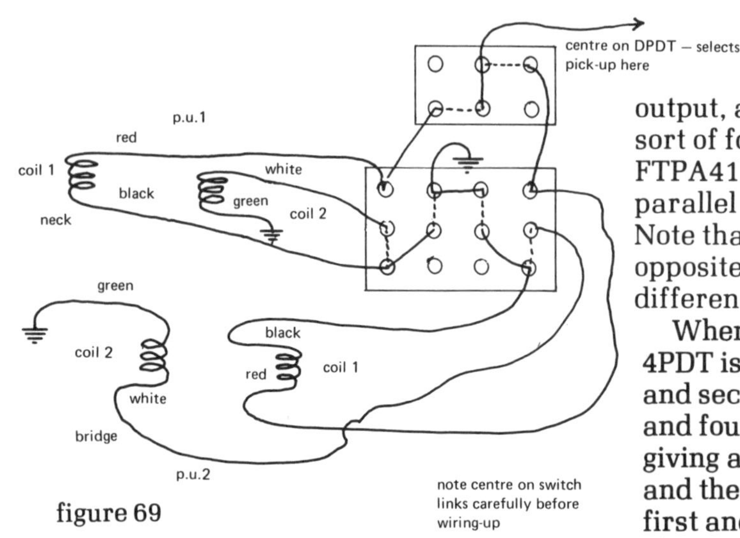

figure 69

consist of two coils, one under first and second strings, the other under third and fourth, such as on the *"Fender" *"Jazz Bass" guitar or *"Fender" *"Precision Bass" guitar. The illustration here shows two J bass pick-ups wired for a mono output, and wired to a centre on 4PDT (a sort of four pole version of the JBT or FTPA41) to give series, single coil, or parallel on both pick-ups simultaneously. Note that the pick-ups should be mounted opposite ways round — this makes no difference to phase by the way.

When both pick-ups are selected, and 4PDT is set to centre, coils 2, under first and second on pick-up 1, and under third and fourth on pick-up 2, will cut out, giving a deeper tone on third and fourth, and the snappier bridge pick-up tone on first and second — ideal for really funky octave playing. In the other settings, the 4PDT gives series or parallel on both pick-ups at once. They can be used together or separately. If two outputs are taken from the DPDT selector switch, instead of the linked mono one shown here, this set-up can be extended to run into two channels or two amps, separating the octaves even further.

A custom built fretless guitar. 'Split-octaves' wiring, push/pull tone cut on volume knob. Series/parallel and active tone switch (DiMarzio unit).

Simple Split Octave Bass

A 4PDT on/on/on is used here as pick-up selector and simultaneous tap switch.

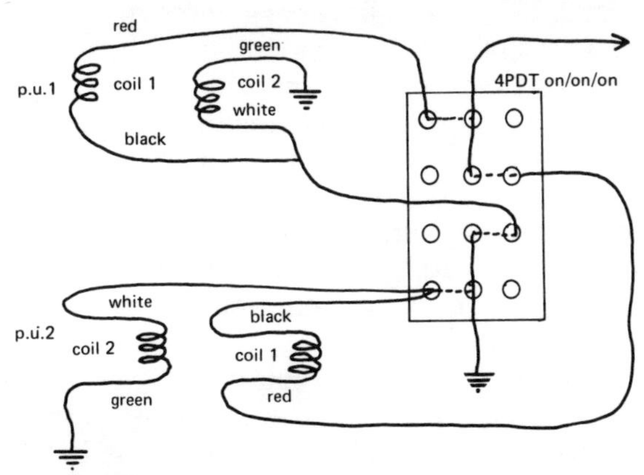

figure 70

When pick-up 1 is selected solo, coil 2 on pick-up 2 will be tapped, to no effect as this pick-up 2 is not on. Conversely, when pick-up 2 is selected, coil 2 on pick-up 1 will be tapped, again to no effect as this pick-up 1 is not on. However, because the switch links the way it does, when both pick-ups are selected, both taps will also be on, so the sounds will come from pick-up 1 coil 1 under third and fourth strings, and from pick-up 2 coil 1 under first and second strings. The advantage is simplicity, the disadvantages, a big volume drop from humbucker solo pick-up to parallel coil mixed pick-ups, and no two humbucker straight mix.

As with the previous split octave wiring, using these colours on, say, a DiMarzio J bass pick-up pair, the bridge pick-up should be mounted back to front, as shown in the drawing.

STENEO *"PRECISION BASS" GUITAR

This bass wiring will separate the pick-up halves for stereo, and is switchable mono/stereo as well as having a series/parallel option in mono. When switched mono it can be used with a normal mono lead. DPDT 2 here will either feed coil 2 into the series/parallel switch, DPDT 1, or flip it out onto the second signal lead in stereo to be fed to another channel or a second amp. Used with the top two strings fed out to a distorted guitar amp gives an unbelievably heavy sound on octaves, and could be well worth considering for use in a rock trio where the extra power could be put to good use. I've certainly found a bass I've wired like this very exciting to play.

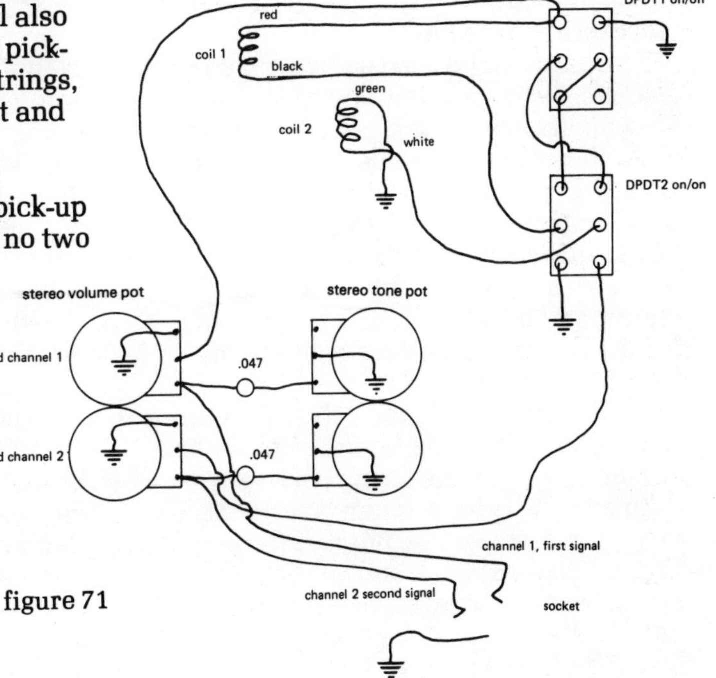

figure 71

KEITH PEGS

Earl Scruggs is generally reckoned to be the man who first used a tuning drop as a bend in a tune to any extent, and this has become a part of bluegrass banjo technique very quickly. Scruggs had trouble getting the pitch back to normal accurately enough fast, and made himself extra pegs with projecting cams that pushed against the string between peg and nut.

Musician, Bill Keith, and Dan Bump of the Beacon Banjo Company (even the names are poetry!) took the whole thing a stage further and designed a banjo peg with integral stops. This is now manufactured by Schaller, and the units are sold in pairs as 'Scruggs' pegs in the U.K.

Tuning is held by friction as in a normal banjo peg, but once a high note has been tuned and the top stop set, and a low note tuned and the low stop set, then the peg will only move between those two points. Maximum change on a tightish plain treble is about a tone and a half, much more on a wound bass.

The pegs can be used on light strung electric, but tuning stability is crucial. Fine tuners are needed to avoid having to reset the stops, and while bridge units with fine tuners are available, they are not always suitable. This is so particularly where the strings run through the bridge to the back of the guitar, and personally, all I want on my bridge is mass and stability, not fiddly bits. There is a specific type of fiddle fine tuner available that is suitable. This tuner does not attach to the fiddle tailpiece, but rather 'floats' on the string between tailpiece and bridge. It can be attached, on guitar, between the nut and the peg barrel. Hooks at each end go round the string, and a central screw can then be used to distort the string to a greater or lesser degree to raise or lower tension.

I have found Keith pegs to work fine on plain trebles, and quite acceptably on bottom strings, though the barrel hole will need to be drilled out to a larger diameter to take the sixth at least. Careful setting is needed, and I find that a brass nut with very smooth finished slot bottoms will allow easy settling to lower notes.

Using Keith pegs, it is possible to drop from standard tuning to at least two open chords quickly and silently, and chord harmonics, played rasgueado, can give a very fair approximation of an auto-harp sound in the hurly-burly of a band mix, among other things. Open bends can sound very rich, but things do not work so well with a capo, which restricts the slacking of the strings.

Tuning problems preclude their use on unstable guitars, and the pegs are sold in pairs with one thick barrel, one thin. Three pairs can be juggled around on guitar to get the most suitable barrel positions. I use, most often; thick first — tone drop; thin second — tone drop; thin third — semitone drop; thick fourth — tone raise; thick fifth — tone drop; thin sixth — tone drop. I've had no problems at all holding pitch, the guitar stays near as possible in tune from string change to string change (the period varies according to funds), and the fine tuners provide ample minor variation. I have found it easier in use, on a double-sided headstock, to run the lower strings round the barrel in the opposite direction to normal in order to keep the drops on the basses in the same direction as the drops on the trebles.

Fitting is simple, they require the same diameter headstock hole as normal Schaller machine-heads, but do not have a locating screw. This is replaced by a spike on the base of the unit that digs into the headstock wood, and grip is supplied by the shaft nut. It is important to consider stop access when fitting.

When fitted and tuned, the peg buttons can be removed and repositioned simply by means of a thumbscrew to get the most convenient angle for quick operation. You will probably encounter problems with your guitar case, the pegs project forty-six millimetres from the headstock wood.

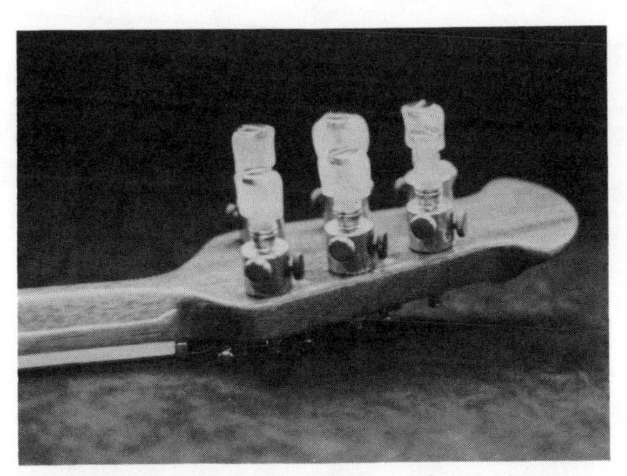

Keith Pegs.

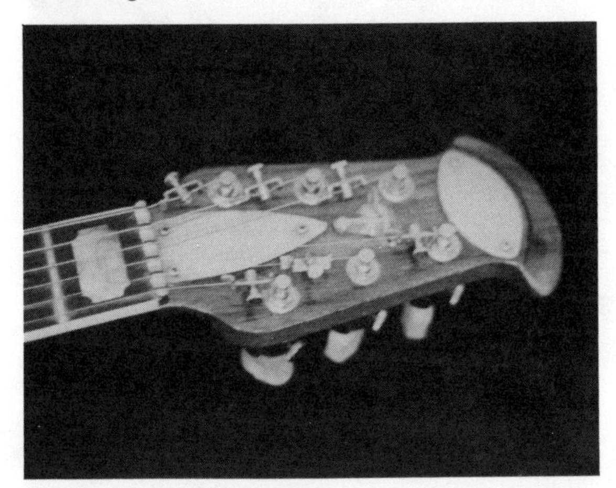

Fiddle floating fine tuners.

CUTTING OUT EXTRA CAVITIES

You might need, at some stage in your customising, to take out wood for an extra pick-up, or a battery cavity. Mark out on the surface the area you are going to cut into, if it's for a pick-up, use the mounting ring you will be using as a template. If it's for a battery, measure the battery, with connector, and transfer the width and length measurements to the surface to be cut. Don't forget that with most pick-ups, a little extra space will be required at each end to accommodate the screw and spring mounting. You can partially mark this through the mounting ring pick-up screw hole.

Measure the required depth on a quarter inch or under drill bit, from the very tip of the cutting edge, and mark it on the bit with an elastic band. Before fitting it into the drill, use it to check finally against the guitar that the bottom of the cavity will not go too close to the outside surface of the guitar, or right through it. Drill out inside the marked area, as far down as the elastic band, checking the depth measurement of the elastic band frequently to make sure it has not been moved further up the bit. Drill the holes as close together as you can without having the drill break out of the hole it is cutting into a neighbouring hole. Do not drill too close to the edge of the marked out area. When the area is filled with holes, cut out the waste wood between the holes with a chisel, or, preferably, a bent gouge. Flatten and smooth the cavity floor with a dog-leg chisel, and take the sides out to the marked edge with a quarter inch chisel. Restrain the chisel when cutting downwards towards the cavity floor, so that you lessen the force behind it when you slip, and lessen the danger of breaking through the floor.

Mahogany or ash is more likely to splinter than maple, so watch out for grain direction on these woods, particularly at corners and when flattening out the cavity floor. I think the dog-leg is essential for the cavity floor, as it lessens the cutting angle. (See Notes — chisels)

File or sand, carefully, any rough finish edges at the cavity edge to avoid accidental tearing up of the finish, and seal the cavity sides and floor with either wood-primer or thinned polyurethane after drilling cable holes.

This is my regular gigging axe, it's over the top and I love it. The possibility that you might think it's unbelievably awful merely confirms the point of customising. It gets bashed about, inevitably, and hurtled all over town on the back of a motorbike, but I've had no problems beyond a broken switch or two — both turned out to be poor quality components. Three months elapsed between the cover photo and this one, so you can see the guitar is slowly evolving as I discover more things I want it to do.

Here, it has three X2Ns with open top cases, a brass scratchplate cut by hand from sheet, brass trim, a fourteen ounce brass bridge sealed up after setting, with engineering penetrating adhesive, strings through from the back of the guitar for extra stability, series/single/parallel on each pick-up plus coil phase reverse and whole pick-up phase reverse on front pick-up and routing on centre pick-up, biased mix, two × mono outputs, onboard pre-amp, cross-top brass knobs are passive volume, bottom left is pre-amp gain, bottom right master tone (cuts before pre-amp) charge socket (black knob between outputs is phono socket cover), rechargeable PP3 housed under rounded brass plate rear bass side of bridge, check lights and cut out switch, strap-locks, copper-sheathed steel saddle springs, flat fingerboard neck (made beautifully by Ovation), DiMarzio wide oval fret-wire, fluted brass nut, Keith pegs and fine tuners, brass control cavity plate at back, and a mercury tilt switch that cuts power when the guitar is stood up. It sounds hilarious to say that the guitar switches itself off, but in actual fact, this device has turned out to be very convenient. It wires in very simply on the battery positive lead, and is taped (at the correct angle) to the inside of the control cavity plate, and saves messing about unplugging or switching amps off when the guitar is put down during a gig.

Building from Parts

Making up a whole guitar for yourself can be immensely satisfying, and done properly and carefully can give you a beautiful instrument, but not necessarily cheaply or easily. Currently, parts are available from different manufacturers that are all to twenty-five and a half inch scale length, and as pick-ups are made to more or less standard size, theoretically you should be able to select from a variety of catalogues the different bits you fancy.

Choosing the bits you need takes careful thought, how much power you need, tonal qualities and so on, and while exotic hardwoods may look good, maple could still sustain better, and so on. Your budget will obviously have a big influence, so careful and thorough costing before you start is important. It is all too easy to underestimate, and fail to allow for things like the solid brass bridge block that can cost more than half as much as a neck, or the complex switch that can cost half as much as a set of machine heads. It's also possible that your existing tool stock will be inadequate.

As this book project was nearing completion, a couple of little deals landed me with enough parts to do up a couple of Strat type custom guitars for myself, I think that running through the story of one of them should give you some idea of what is involved.

The first guitar was to be based on a DiMarzio mahogany/paduak/maple body and Mighty Mite maple/ebony/ neck. The body was secondhand, and holes for two pots and a selector switch had already been drilled — no problem, they were pretty well where I would have put them anyway. Both body and neck had a good primary coat on that I reckoned was good enough to last a while without my adding to it. The neck was actually fairly fat already, and I didn't want to make it any fatter. The body was routed to take two humbuckers and a tremolo bridge, and holes had been drilled at manufacture for the six top bridge screws and for the neck. A black plastic control compartment plate was also supplied.

First I intended to fit the bridge, a solid brass unit. The two large holes for the big screws which hold on the tremolo spring catch plate were not drilled. I marked my drill points using the plate holes, and drilled about one and a quarter inches towards the neck and inside the spring routing, using a small Leytool single-handled drill. This Leytool is ideal for this, as there are no projections and the plastic casing can be held quite flat against the body without fear of anything damaging the wood. I smeared Vaseline on the ends of the screws (butter is more traditional!) and mounted the unit. I fitted the bridge with six roundhead (not countersunk) screws. The holes on the base of the unit were not deep enough to take the whole length of the straight hooks of the tremolo springs, so I trimmed one mm off each hook, using music-wire grade sidecutters, rather than drilling deeper into the brass, as I judged that there was still plenty of grip. The sidecutters are important, music-wire grade cutters have a much harder cutting edge, less hard edges will be damaged (see Notes). I mounted the springs, using a buttonhook to stretch them out to attach them. I now fitted the string earth. I used a length of single strand, somewhere under half a millimetre thick, wire, scavenged from the unswept site of a mains socket installation. I cut enough to run from the spring catching bar into the control compartment and right round it to give me a convenient earth rail. I soldered the end of the wire to the spring bar using a 430 degrees C iron. This is an important point, bad string earthing is a common fault on this type of guitar and is a source of diabolical hum and noise. You can diagnose the fault by the fact of a decrease in noise when your hand is in contact with the strings. A good solder joint here is essential, merely tangling the wire with the springs will not give a good enough contact. A run of the mill twenty-five watt soldering iron may well not give enough heat to get solder to take on this big a lump of cold metal. If you do not own a hot enough iron, you will probably have to ask for help at your local electrical repair shop, or possibly you might ask your dealer to help with this when you buy the parts, assuming he has a repair facility.

I'd decided to do all the bodywork first before attaching the neck, simply for ease of handling, and my next step was to mount the pick-ups. On this guitar I was using DiMarzio X2Ns. I favour powerful pick-ups, not so much for the distortion, but because they will stand more drop from the loading effects of various parallel mixes, and will stand a cut to utilise the effects of a .001 capacitor volume pot bypass. I find the Schecter Superock quite similar to the X2N, but it is smoother, and lacks the honky little high mid peak of the X2N which I find helps me get what I want tonally in a couple of mixes. I also go for a bar pick-up as I bend a lot within chords, and consequently find it fairly essential to avoid the drop-out normally found with individual poles. I have never really found an insurmountable string balance problem with either the X2N or the Schecter, or the Lawrence L500 for that matter, but that could be that I'm so used to bar pick-ups I compensate unconsciously.

I fitted the pick-ups into brass covers, pushing them down into the covers firmly, and clamping them in while I tapped the excess edges of the covers in over the pick-up base slightly and soldered the join. It is important to earth covers properly, or they will not shield effectively, but will rather contribute to noise. The pick-up base, where it is metal, is normally connected to the conductor shield. I then put the front pick-up into its mounting ring, having cut the spring to the appropriate length, guessed from experience, tried it all in the front slot and jiggled it till I was sure I'd got it central. I then marked and drilled the four corner holes for the mounting ring screws, threaded the cable through, and fitted the unit. I pulled the cable right through the control compartment, and taped it to the back of the guitar with masking tape, writing 'front' on the tape with felt tip. I followed the same procedure with the back pick-up, taping its cable to the back of the guitar marked 'back'. Remember, with identical pick-ups, you can't tell one cable from t'other when they're both sticking out of the same hole.

I tried the socket, a good quality one salvaged from a wrecked effects pedal, for size, and fitted it to a flexible plastic four hole plate. I put it in a comfortable position in the hole in the guitar body, and marked and drilled the socket plate holes. I soldered positive and earth wires to the socket, threaded them through into the control compartment, and mounted the socket and plate. The flexible plate settled smoothly to the curve of the guitar edge.

Next I fitted a 500k audio volume pot, and a push-pull tone pot with a switch facility. I fitted a box type three-way selector, with a brass rhythm treble plate. The barrel of the switch was too thick for both plate and body holes, I reamed them out using a cello peg-head reamer. (See Notes)

I took the front pick-up four conductor cable, and soldered red to the top leg of the three-way switch, and soldered green and shield to the earth rail. I took the black and white, twisted them together, and soldered them to one leg of one of the two pairs of contacts at the bottom of the push-pull pot switch. I soldered from the other one of this pair to the earth rail. This would give me a pull out coil tap on the front pick-up.

I then soldered a wire from the centre leg of the three-way to the wiper of the volume pot together with one wire from a .001 capacitor, heatsinking the capacitor wire with clamping forceps (see Notes). I then soldered the other wire of the .001 to the output leg of the volume pot, together with the positive wire I had previously soldered to the jack socket. I earthed the other volume pot leg via the earth rail, and earthed the casing. I then soldered a .02 capacitor from the wiper of the tone pot to earth, and soldered a wire from the input leg of the tone pot to the output leg of the volume pot with the .001 and socket wire already there.

I soldered the red from the back pick-up to the bottom terminal of the three-way, the green and shield to the earth rail, twisted together the black and white and soldered them to the spare leg of the tone pot to get a partial nine-ten tap via the .02 on the wiper. I linked from the spare leg connection to one of the other bottom pair of terminals on the push-pull pot switch, and earthed its fellow. This gave me complete tap simultaneously with the front pick-up when the tone knob was pulled out. I then tested by plugging into an amp and tapping the pick-up covers, it all worked, and waggling it all about showed no signs of dry joints or fluffed connections. When I first started doing this sort of thing, that would have been something of a miracle, but with a bit of practice and thought, you can come to expect to get it right first time so that if it doesn't work, you start looking for a component fault. A failed capacitor is a common one, and is often caused by overheating during soldering without adequate heatsinks.

I fitted the brass knob to the tone pot with no problem, it had a solid shaft, but the volume pot had a split shaft designed for push on knobs rather than the type I had here, which secured by means of a small worm. I filled the split with a piece of brass cut to size, and fitted the knob. It is important to fill the split because otherwise the worm may distort or break a piece of the shaft, or sometimes may simply disappear into the split without gaining any grip. If you break the shaft, you have to replace the pot. The X2Ns incidentally have to be mounted the right way round, so choice of type of tap is the only means of deciding which coil to drop out for tap sounds. The reason for the specific mounting is that the extra magnets in the base of the pick-up are cut away under fifth and sixth string to minimise string pull. Using red as hot, the earth type taps take out the rear coil.

I then fitted Schallers to the headstock, and a brass nut, fluting and finishing it, partially cutting the depth of the string slots. I had tried mating neck and body before, and found the neck butt too thick. I now shaved it down, where it would be in contact in the joint, with a sharp knife. I put it in, and checking side to side alignment with a thirty inch straightedge (see Notes), I marked the drill holes with a thin scribe through the holes already in the body and drilled them. I then greased the screws as before, and with a brass neck plate, mounted the neck, tightening up with a T handle pozidrive. I regard the T handle driver, bought for £1 from the Earls Court motorbike show, as an essential for this job, as it does them up hard and tight without danger of slipping and fouling up the screw heads. I strung up, and using a small scribe, marked the holes for the two small string catches that hold the top four strings hard against the nut. I drilled them and fitted the catches, and tuned the guitar up to concert pitch. I checked the neck relief out at just under ten thou. without adjustment, and left it there. I then completed the cutting of the depth of the nut slots and got the action right that end. The neck pitch proved to be within the range of adjustment at the saddles, so I set intonation roughly, set pick-up and action height and set intonation fine. I fitted brass strap buttons, the bottom end one offset towards the bass side to give a better hang.

I didn't like the look of the black plastic control compartment cover, so I took it off and, using it as a template, cut another out of a piece of brass sheet, with an electric jigsaw. I filed the edges down square, buffed and polished the piece after drilling and countersinking the screwholes, attached an earth wire to it via one of the screw holes in the body, and fitted it. I had to use tape around the inside edges of the plate to get it flush with the back of the body.

The finished job is undoubtedly a lovely guitar. It has a good range of tone, sustains well and evenly, feels good and looks good, and was worth all the effort and expense. You can see from the story what it took and what I needed, on top of a few pozidrives, that can't just be borrowed for the occasion from the plumber over the road. Each special tool should be read as a possible hitch in construction.

The second guitar was a much less complicated affair mainly because it was basically a single pick-up rock guitar without frills. I used a Lawrence L500 for it to get a raw edge to the sound, and tapped it via the tone control spare leg and .02 capacitor from wiper to earth.

The Ash body I finished by hand using melamine, and getting the coats on, together with the rubbing down and buffing added considerably to overall building time. I had once again to shave the neck down to fit into the body join, and I broke a strap button screw on the last few turns because I had failed to drill first. Don't assume, as I did, wrongly, that because it was going into end grain it would go in easily. I had the greatest of difficulty getting it out, and thought I would have learnt by now.

The most interesting problem on this guitar was related to string spacing. Although there was space between the saddles on the Schecter bridge unit, the strings would not sit in close enough together to go over the bar poles on the Lawrence pick-up. I solved the problem by aligning the neck and pick-up with the sixth, which brought the sixth over the bass side tip of the bar, and then forcing the first saddle over so that the saddles bunched together. I then drilled a small hole into the base plate of the bridge, after I'd set intonation, into which the outer leg/worm of the first saddle fitted. This arrangement prevented it slipping.

I had no other problems with the assembly of the guitar, and am very satisfied with the performance and feel of it.

These two are actually fairly expensive guitars, but much cheaper Jap parts are available, and I've seen perfectly good playable guitars put together by essentially amateur hands. I don't see why, given a little commonsense, a bit of advice, and reasonable tools, building from parts can't be done by anybody.

Notes

A — on the back of a pot, along with part number, indicates that that pot is linear. That is, the rate of change of the resistance is even. As a volume pot, not a lot of use with the .001 capacitor where the treble lift on decreasing volume is required. I found linear volume pots very ineffective immediately in front of a pre-amp in the guitar. There tends to be less treble loss noticeable with linear pots. I have found a 250k linear effectve as a tone control in several guitars, but 500k linear has proved unsatisfactory

Action — see Basic set-up.

Audio — the rate of resistance changes at a rate tapered to match the uneveness of human audial perception — that is, because the change is uneven, you hear it as even.

B — on the back of a pot with part number, indicates a resistance which changes at a logarithmic rate. Gives a similar effect in use to audio.

Buffing soap — available at good toolshops and hardware shops. Can be used by hand on leather to take out fine scratches on brass, or as part of fret buffing job. Is designed specifically for buffing wheel. See 'Frets'.

Capacitor — value measured in microfarads. For example .05 mf, or .022 mf. Sometimes, just the figure is printed on the unit, with maker's logo and voltage rating. Voltage rating is unimportant from point of view of use in guitars, but higher voltage units tend to be tougher, and harder to damage by overheating. See 'How Pick-up and Pots Work'.

Increasingly now, capacitors are available with the value given in pico-farads, or pf, and in a three figure code. The first two figures denote value, and the third is a multiplier, or the number of zeroes. Thus 472 = 47 and 2 zeroes, or 4700 pf, corresponding to .0047 microfarads (mf). Similarly, 473 would be 47,000 picfarads, or .047 microfarads -which would be a fairly deep cutting tone control capacitor.

Sometimes, capacitor values may be given in nano-farads. E.g., a .001 microfarads capacitor could be called I nano-farad, or 1000 picofarads (that would be 102 in three figure code); a .0047 microfarads could be called 4.7 nano-fards, or 4n7, or 4700 pf.

So, 1000 pf = Inf
1000 nf = Imf

I would recommend that you make up a tag board with a range of capacitors mounted on it for try-out purposes. The lowest cut you'll need will be .068 mf, and this value bears mainly on basses. Guitar tone control values can vary from .05 mf to .01 mf. Beyond this point, you will find some interesting tone variations on partial taps from 6800 pf to 680 pf, where the lighter cut from the tapped coil can give some subtle but valuable tone shadings. I usually try out as far as 180 pf as a matter of course, which has a minimal effect on anything but the most trebly humbucker. You may also find some benefit in experimenting with volume pot treble bypass capacitor value. I suggest .001 mf as routine, but if you find this too harsh, halve it and go for 500 pf, or a few notches either side depending on how low a bypass threshold you find satisfactory.

The tag board should have the connections up oneside soldered together, so that only one connector has to be moved to different capacitors. The connector leads should have either spring hook probes or very fine crocodile clips at the guitar end, and these you will hook into the contacts where you will eventually solder the capacitor you decide on. At the tagboard end of the leads, you need crocodile clips that will attach to the tags without touching the test capacitor's neighbour.

Cyanoacrilate — bionic glue. See 'Glues'.

Chisels — dog-leg, particularly suitable for working on floor of cavity. Spoon bit gouge — useful for opening out and extending interior routing without disturbing cover plate recess. Eventually will wear to back-bent gouge, also handy for interior work, as are straight and bent gouges. See photograph p. 59 and 'Cutting out extra cavities'

Conductors — see 'Pick-Up Basics'. The wires that run from pick-up coils to controls.

DPDT — see SPDT. Double Pole Double Throw. Works like two SPDTs in one box and one toggle. On/on/on DPDTs see page 32. Similiarly, 4PDT = Four Pole Double Throw.

Epoxy — see 'Glues and Finishes'.

FTPA41 — see page 32. On/on/on DPDT switch.
Made by the New Ohto Switch Co., Japan, the 4 refers to the triangulated paddle style toggle. Other toggle styles can be obtained. If you have difficulty getting hold of suitable switches, contact House of Power, Electron House, Cray Avenue, St Mary Cray, Orpington Kent BR5 3QJ, telephone Orpington (66) 71531. I have been assured that a switch expert there will deal sympathetically with frustrated customisers. They carry the Alco range of mini toggles, and the Alco equivalent to the FTPA*I (*depends on toggle style remember) is the MTM206PA. Conversely, the Ohto equivalent to the Alco MTA406PA on/on/on 4PDT would be F4TPA21, where the second digit indicates the 4 pole nature."

Forceps — see 'Wiring' page 20. Available from Bell and Croydon, Wigmore Street, London W.1., or ask your doctor for his local supplier. May be available in electrical parts shop. Keep an eye on local markets, some hospitals sell off old ones to junk dealers, though very often these may be slightly weakened by heat involved in sterilisation.

Forceps are available from Toolrange and other component suppliers, but I have found that I can get excellent quality Government surplus ones from Laurence Corner's Boffin Shop, Drummond Steet, London NW1, at around half the component suppliers' list prices.

Standard(ish) Spencer forceps are the most commonly available, but they can be had with a bent nose, and various shape larger tissue forceps can come in useful for getting bits and pieces back into F-hole guitars without having to pull the bits back in with bits of string or wires soldered to switch-toggles and pots shafts.

Tonsil forceps have a serrated grip nose which is curved nearly into a semi-circle, and these can be useful for holding a component during soldering and simultaneously shielding it from the hot iron end.

Fret Files — see 'Frets'. Your local dealer can order them for you from Stentor.

Measurements — throughout the book are given in the forms used most commonly, and which are actually the most convenient. Relief is talked of in

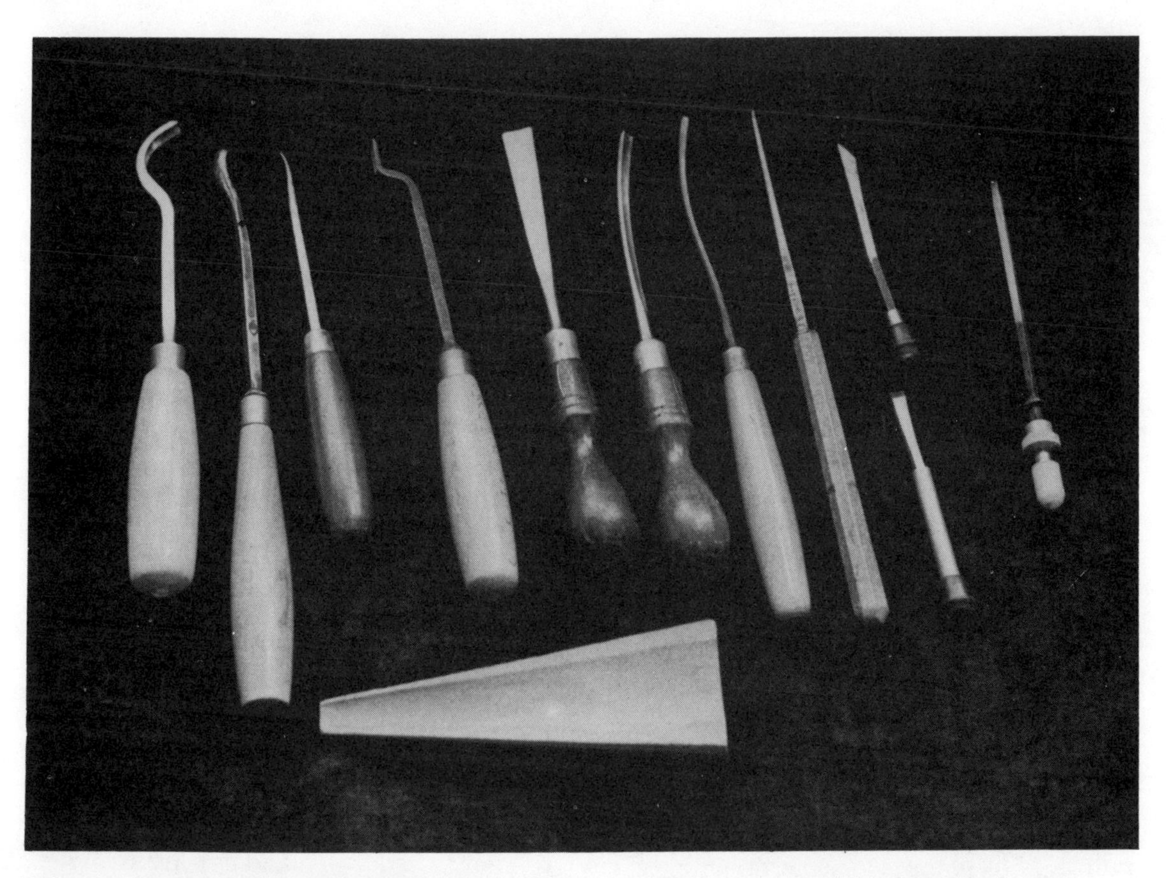

Left to right: Spoon-bit gouge, half worn spoon bit, back-bent gouge, ¼″ dog-leg chisel, gouge, bent gouge, fine bent gouge, veiner (very fine straight gouge), two small chisels ground from broken carving chisels, ⅛″ chisel with end ground thinner. *Bottom:* gouges stone.

thousandths of an inch, variation in correctly set necks is usually between five thou. and fifteen thou., and the units have a convenient spread. Similiarly, most of us have been brought up on 25½ inch scale, or 24¾ inch scale. These two are almost class names now, and their implications relate directly to how we know a given string gauge will feel to bend. Action height is given in millimetres because absolute minimum on the first is one mm, and general maximum before things get difficult in high positions is two mm. Over that height, and we know something is wrong. So a 1.2 mm first would be nice and light, but not to be hit too hard on a bend. Converted, it reads as .047 inches (which measurement to me means a thickish sixth) or slightly over 3/64 inch (which means nothing to me). One mm and two mm give definite stops.

Conversion is simple. Multiply millimetres by .03937 to get inches, divide inches by .03937 to get millimetres.

Thus 25½ inches divided by .03937 = 647.7 mm, or just under a 65 centimetre scale. Conversely, a 63 centimetre scale is 630 mm divided by .03937 = 24.8031 inches, or roughly a 24¾ scale.

Melamine — see 'Glues and Finishes'. Available from F.T. Morell, 214, Acton Lane, London NW10 7NH, or Mill Lane, Woodley, Stockport, Cheshire (061-430 2292), in minimum five litre quantities. It is available Gloss, Satin, Semi Matt, or Matt.

Needlefiles — see 'The Nut'.

Pot — strictly speaking, is incorrect slang for volume or tone control variable resistor. It is short for potentiometer. The volume or tone pot consists of a casing and shaft. Inside the casing is an incomplete circle of carbon, the ends of which are connected to the two outside legs or tags to which the guitar wiring is attached. The wiper is connected physically, but not electrically, to the rotating shaft, and moves round in contact with the carbon track. The wiper is connected electrically to the middle leg or tag of the pot. The pot gets noisy when the carbon track and wiper get dirty. The carbon track is the resistance, and the wiper makes contact so that variable amounts of resistance are brought into the circuit. See 'How Pick-Ups and Pots work', and Notes on A and Audio.

Pot shafts — choice of type if available can be important — see 'Building from Parts'.

Pot values — values are not critical in a guitar. 250k ohms is associated with single coil guitars, and 500k ohms with double coil guitars. In fact, I have seen recent "Fenders" with one meg ohm pots fitted. Generally, I would recommend from 500k to one meg for most purposes. one meg is thought to be more likely to prevent any treble leakage to earth. As far as tone controls are concerned, you should experiment to find the best set-up that will suit you — individual taste can vary a great deal in this area. Personally, I found that after trying half a dozen different pots in my Ovation Preacher, I ended up using one of the factory fitted pair, but with a .033 capacitor. This however, is a guitar that now produces a phenomenal amount of treble quite naturally as, partially, a result of considerable physical modification.

Reamers — see tools, photograph p. 63. Violin and cello peghead reamers have been used on guitars for opening out machine head holes to take a larger barrelled machine head than fitted at manufacture, and generally these are available with T handles. Both sizes are usually needed for headstock conversion. A single reamer specifically for this job is also available from Stentor via your dealer, or mail order from Touchstone Tonewoods Ltd., 27 Lesbourne Road, Reigate RH2 7JS. This one has a squared end for use with either a tap-handle or a brace. If you're keeping an eye out on a local market, generally you need one that runs from just over a quarter inch to just under an half inch, for guitar machine heads.

The violin and cello peghead reamers particularly also have applications for opening out pot and switch holes for larger units, and you may well find smaller reamers come in handy. Your local toolshop will be able to advise on suitable reamers for jobs like opening out the mounting holes on bridges and so on.

It is essential to maintain a consistent torque and downward pressure on a reamer in order to avoid getting an oval or otherwise distorted hole. Always mark slightly early on the taper, with an elastic band, your maximum required hole diameter, so that you can do the last stages alternately cutting and trying for fit, to avoid oversizing the hole unnecessarily.

Be warned, good reamers can be expensive, and if only a one-off job is involved, perhaps you should seek professional help.

Relief — see 'Basic Set-up'.

Shellac — purified lac. Lac is exuded by lac insects and found as an incrustation on Banyan and Fig trees. Shellac, dissolved in methylated spirit, forms the basis of French polish. It is available in flake form, or stick form, or as a shellac stopper from F.T. Morrell. The sticks can be had from Stentor, and flakes from a fine art shop, or sculptor's supplier.

The shellac is cut off from the stick and

applied with a hot knife, and will fill small dents, or fingerboard tears. It is also used for filling fret end saw cuts. The flakes are primarily for dissolving, but can be melted into a block, or melted individually on the site of a small dent. If you heat it on a knife blade over a flame, do not let it catch fire, as it will go to cinders. It is available in colours, a black that will go with ebony, and various browns that should match most fingerboards.

Silicone grease — is available in aerosol form for lubricating pots and switches after cleaning with aerosol cleaning fluid. In some preparations, the two actions are combined. Many pots have spray access via a hole through which the connectors project. Sealed pots are lifetime lubricated, theoretically anyway.

Silicone rubber — available in tubes, is used for protecting delicate electrical assemblies by 'potting', that is, putting the parts in silicone rubber in a box. It can also be useful for curing small internal rattles, it sets to a rubbery texture. It can be pulled off finishes when set without damage. Note for household use, it smells unpleasant.

Silicone polish — best never used on a guitar, it makes finish touch-ups extremely difficult as lacquer will not stick where it has been used.

Silica gel — moisture absorbent crystals. The stuff in guitars and cases in little bags when new. Useful for storage. Can be re-used after heating, which releases contained absorbed moisture. Available from good chemists.

Straight edges — It is better to use one that is designed specifically as a straight edge rather than the edge of a rule, which may confuse the issue by flexing.

Maun straight edges are available from most decent toolsphops, and at fair enough prices — a matter of a few pounds a time. An eighteen inch will do nicely for relief on guitars and basses, and a thirty inch is useful for neck alignment and so on.

I think it is advisable to round off the corners to minimise possible damage from accidental knocks.

In case of difficulty finding a local supplier, contact Maun Industries in Mansfield, Nottingham.

SPDT — Single Pole Double Throw. A type of switch, where the signal from (or to) a wire connected to the centre leg can be thrown to (or taken from) either of two outer legs where the switch is on/on, where on/off/on, contact is made with neither in the centre position.

On/on SPDT

on/off/on DPDT

on/on 4PDT

Strap locking devices — the type pictured below has a socket, mounted on the guitar in place of the usual strap knob, into which plugs the gadget attached to the strap by washers and circlips. Release is effected by pushing the knob in the outside centre of the strap part of the assembly.

An alternative type fits over a rimmed knob on the guitar, and release is effected by pulling out a central stop. I have found the former very reliable, but have been worried about breaking my nails with the latter, as the knob that you pull out can get slippy.

Both types affix permanently to the strap, and it is best to glue up the slotted opening in the strap to prevent any long term possibility of it stretching enough to allow the strap assembly to ease out, as you will quickly get to rely on the strap to take all the weight of the guitar.

The socket type pictured here can be sunk into the wood of the body quite successfully, the top rim is slightly larger than the bottom, so a washer can be fitted to cover any finish marking at the lip of the drilled hole.

Strap locking device.

String earthing — see 'Building from Parts'.

Test Equipment — for testing part-wired guitars and checking out unwired pick-ups, remove the jack plug from one end of a guitar lead, and replace it with crocodile clips on signal wire and shield, or with clip-on probes. You can then, for example, clip on to an unfitted pick-up to see which coils are affected by what taps. If you take a four conductor, clip red into the signal crocodile clip, and green into shield clip, twisting black and white together will give series wiring, and touching black and white against the shield crocodile clip will give an earth type tap. By tapping gently on the coils with the lead plugged into a amp you will be able to hear which coil has been turned off, and mount your pick-up the way round you want this to happen in the guitar . See photograph p.56.

For checking switch centre links, you need two small clip-on probes, a 1.5 volt battery, a 1.5 volt torch bulb and holder, and a small length of wire. Connect from one probe to battery negative, from battery positive to bulb holder, from bulb holder other contact to the other probe, and you can attach the probes to switch legs to see which ones make contact in different switch positions.

Multimeters are useful, for checking out coils, pot values, battery levels and so on, but can be expensive. You could try looking around for a cheaper Russian job. Generally, these have been cheaper because the Russians have been very keen to get hold of foreign currency rather than because of inferior quality. I have used a Russian meter for quite a while with no problems, and while it may not have the same charisma as an Avo-meter or similiar, it has proved quite adequate, and accurate, for my needs. Get as much different advice as you can if you're considering this sort of purchase. Different dealers may have different axes to grind, and in this area you may well not be able to tell sound advice from a sales pitch.

If you feel that your budget will stand a professional quality meter, I can say that I have been very happy with a Fluke 8024B digital multimeter. The 1982 list price including tax was a hefty £180.90. Apart from the on-stage safety aspect of getting reliable voltage difference readings between different amp chassis, the unit has a few extra applications that suit a customiser. It will read a.c. millivolts

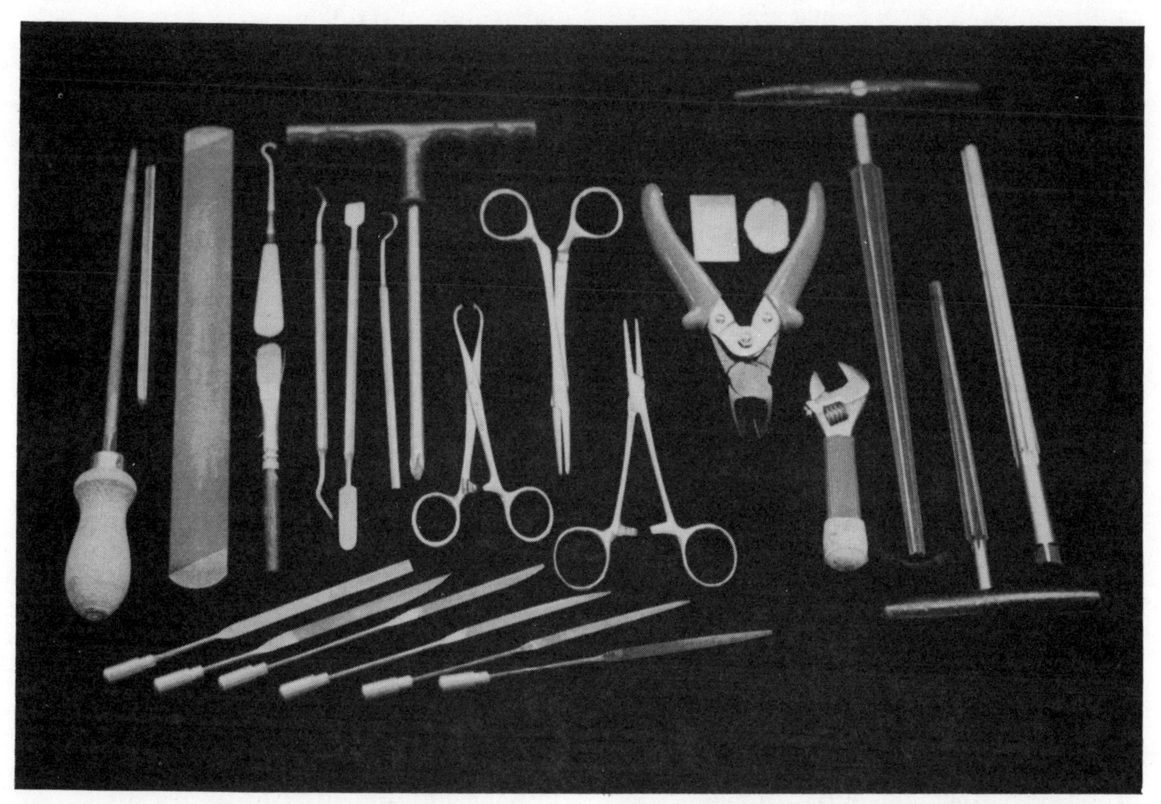

accurately and give a precise indication of passive guitar output, and has a peak hold facility that will register and continue to show the initial wallop coming off a guitar as the note is struck - these measurements have a bearing on distortion occuring in a pre-amp, onboard or in your amplifier, and though obviously output will vary considerably depending on how hard you actually hit the strings, you will find it that much easier to make objective comparative evaluations of pick-ups. The unit also offers continuity and conductance indications, and resistance up to 20 meg ohms without the need for an extra power supply. Contact Fluke G.B. Ltd., Colonial Way, Watford, Herts., tel: 0923 40511 for info."

Tools — see photograph above. Left to right: Rat-tail file; concave fret-file; ten inch fine single cut with ground-off tang and corners; button-hook for lifting strings out of fret-slots, and small clean-up brush; dental tools for fine scraping, gluing etc; T-bar pozidrive; claw-end forceps for pulling cable through, fishing bits out etc.; thickish nose forceps for soldering; thinner nose forceps; heavy duty compound action side cutters; small adjustable spanner; 'cello peg-head reamer; violin peg-head reamer; guitar machine-head reamer.
Bottom: Needlefiles, the small brass ends stop the tang end from digging into my palm.

Tool Suppliers.

If you have trouble tracking down what you need locally, here are a couple of firms that supply by post.

Toolrange Ltd, Upton Road, Reading, Berks RG34JA, tel: 0734 29446. Toolrange carry an excellent range of electronics tools and some light engineering tools. They have a wide range of irons (including my favourite Ungarmatic station), and the best selection of small specialised pliers I've seen, including Belzer, Bahco, Xcelite, CK, Lindstrom and more. Items I find extemely useful are the Belzer 2656 end-cutters, the Xcelite 413 small wire-strippers, Bahco 40993 snipe nose with cutter, Lindstrom 3873 curved snipe pliers, CK3786 off-set end-cutters, and Linstrom 3508 flushcutting nippers. Be warned though, that represents over fifty quids' worth. Toolrange carry solder-suckers, essential for re-wiring and replacing components.

Akron Tool Supply Co., 21 Cherry Tree Rise, Buckhurst Hill, Essex IG9 6EB, telephone, 01 505 8135, are good for engineering type tools, drills, grinders, taps & dies and so on. If you're interested in keeping a more systematic eye on your string gauges, they have a good selection of reasonably priced micrometers. The Moore and Wright I outside micrometer has always been good value, but if you can run to £40.00 plus, have a look at the Mitutoyu "Combi-Mike", which can give an English sleeve with Vernier, and Metric digital readout (or vice-versa). Here I might say that although tool prices can seem heavy, remember that properly cared for, decent quality tools will probably outlast you, and expenses incurred in maintaining and improving your instrument are legitimate things for a musician to claim against tax.

J. Simble and Sons, Queens Road, Watford, Herts WD1 2LD tel: Watford 26052, offer a fair enough value for money service that could compensate for a total lack of a local toolshop. The catalogue is well worth a look — number 7 cost .75p."

Wiper — the contact that moves round over the carbon track (resistance) inside a pot — it is connected to the centre leg. See 'How Pick-up and Pots Work'.

Wire cutters — I have found a very small pair of side cutters useful for trimming wire ends and tidying up in a small space like a control compartment, but for heavier work, you need music-wire grade, or piano-wire grade, side cutters. It is well worth buying a pair of heavy duty, compound action, double jointed, sprung side cutters, quite a mouthful for a tool that is powerful enough to be very versatile. The increased cutting power that is available via the gearing means that the cutters can be used for jobs like trimming small pieces of sheet brass to rough shape before filing, where ordinary single action cutters would be useless, and tin-shears too unwieldy. See photograph If you have difficulty getting them from a toolshop. Contact Maun Industries Ltd., Moor Lane, Mansfield, Notts NG18 5SE, tel: Mansfield (0623) 24525

Work area — you may find it difficult to set aside an area for long enough for extensive work, or glue or finish jobs that must be left undisturbed for a period.

However, you must have a firm, padded surface to work properly. Padding is best done with foam-backed carpet with a top covering of felt, and where you cannot tack it down, secure the edges with wide tape. Keep the carpet clean and free from little bits of sharp material such as string ends, brass or fret trimmings, and spilt solder.

In a family home, children must be kept well away from hot soldering irons, cyanoacrilates and finishes, and these and sharp tools must be stored under lock and key. You should make sure that everyone else in the home knows what you are doing — awareness helps avoid accidents, either to individuals or your guitar.